T0116855

PRAYERS FROM THE BIBLE
in Classic Verse

· JAMES VASQUEZ ·

WestBow
PRESS
A DIVISION OF THOMAS NELSON

Copyright © 2011 by James Vasquez.

All rights reserved. No part of this book may be used or reproduced by any means, graphic, electronic, or mechanical, including photocopying, recording, taping or by any information storage retrieval system without the written permission of the publisher except in the case of brief quotations embodied in critical articles and reviews.

WestBow Press books may be ordered through booksellers or by contacting:

WestBow Press
A Division of Thomas Nelson
1663 Liberty Drive
Bloomington, IN 47403
www.westbowpress.com
1-(866) 928-1240

Because of the dynamic nature of the Internet, any web addresses or links contained in this book may have changed since publication and may no longer be valid. The views expressed in this work are solely those of the author and do not necessarily reflect the views of the publisher, and the publisher hereby disclaims any responsibility for them.

Any people depicted in stock imagery provided by Thinkstock are models, and such images are being used for illustrative purposes only.

Certain stock imagery © Thinkstock.

ISBN: 978-1-4497-2779-6 (sc)
ISBN: 978-1-4497-2780-2 (hc)
ISBN: 978-1-4497-2778-9 (e)

Library of Congress Control Number: 2011917924

Printed in the United States of America

WestBow Press rev. date: 10/21/2011

CONTENTS

The Old Testament

The New Testament

ACKNOWLEDGMENTS

Some of these poems have been published in other books by the author (see following page), in whole or part.

This book is dedicated with heartfelt thanks to:

> My children, whose sincerity, faith and thankfulness in prayer since childhood have been such an inspiration to me: Jody, Debbie, David

> Those I joined in small groups to study the Scriptures and pray—In Pasadena, Costa Rica, Colombia, Seattle, Ellensburg

Special thanks to Ruth McHaney Danner for expert editorial assistance.

Biblical quotations are from the New International Version of the Bible, unless otherwise indicated.

ALSO BY JAMES VASQUEZ

Women of the Bible: Their Stories in Verse
(2005)

Men Who Knew Jesus Well
Their Stories in Verse
(2009)

Women of the Bible
Their Stories in Verse
(2d ed., 2009)

Prophets of the Bible
A Classic Collection of Biblical Heroes in Verse
(2009)

Words Jesus Spoke—In Verse
(2010)

The Psalms—In Verse
(2011)

INTRODUCTION

The Bible provides an incredible amount of information about prayer. Indeed, the only reason we can believe the volume of information on prayer is that it's there, written on the pages so clearly.

The Bible teaches about prayer in many ways. From the pages of Scripture we have such helpful instruction as:
- How to pray: without ceasing, in faith, submissively, acknowledging sinfulness,
- When: at all times, early and late day, nighttime, "on all occasions,"
- Where: in private (the closet), in church (the temple), the riverside, the countryside,
- Why: God commands us to pray, the example of Jesus, our own and others' needs,
- For whom and for what: God's blessing, to resist temptation, perseverance, friends who are sick,
- With whom: small and large groups, spouse,
- How *not* to pray: babbling, to be seen or heard by others, self-righteously, with many words.

Thus, the Bible is a virtual handbook on prayer and the question that remains is: given this rich resource on prayer, why do not more Christians pray faithfully? From the testimony of friends and acquaintances over the several decades since I was ordained, and from my own experience,

I believe many—if not most—Christians feel an emptiness in their lives, even guilt, because they pray so little.

In this book of forty-five poems I will address one very helpful practice we should observe for faithful and effective praying: that of following Scriptural examples of prayers uttered by God's people. After all, when the apostles asked Jesus to teach them to pray, he gave them a model. I have chosen most of the major prayers (excluding the Psalms, published in a separate collection), and many briefer, "minor" prayers, to put into verse. Each is preceded by a brief explanation of the context for the prayer, that is, an explanation of what the motivation or inspiration was for the prayer. To understand the true intent of a prayer it is most helpful when we are able to connect the content with the context. A few poems are based not on actual prayers but on passages that teach about prayer. I consider them so helpful they deserve a place in this book.

One might ask, why put the prayers into verse? First, many Old Testament prayers were originally written in Hebrew verse, especially the psalms and others in "The Writings," and though English versions of the Bible attempt to show this form by putting the lines in poetic format, the result hardly suggests true classic poetry in format or rhyme. Second, the prayers are put into verse for the purpose of literary elegance, for I believe rhyming, well-metered poems are pleasing when read to oneself, and especially pleasing when read aloud. Rhyming poetry also aids significantly in memorizing. And third, it's because that's what I do.

James Vasquez, MDiv, PhD
Spokane, WA

Job – "In Dust and Ash"

(JOB 42)

Job has lost his family (ten children, most grown if not all) to a windstorm, his possessions to raiders, sheep to "fire . . . from the sky." His body broke out in sores, and his wife told him to curse God and die. Friends came and saw him, then mourned and offered several explanations for the tragic events, but no real consolation. Job does not blame God for his misfortune—though almost. He finally declares he does not deserve what befell him. Then God speaks to him, reminding him from creation events of God's wisdom, might and sovereignty. We begin with God's words to him. Then Job prays.

Then from a mighty storm God spoke,
"I answer to no man,
But now these questions I will ask,
And answer if you can.

"For who is this of darkened lore,
Of unenlightened mind?
Now brace yourself and offer me
The answer that you find.

"And where were you when earth received
Its firm foundation laid,
From sun by day and moon by night,
Its light and shadows made?

"And tell me if you understand,
Who set its cornerstone,
When all the morning stars rejoiced
With angels round God's throne?

"And who addressed the mighty seas,
Forbidding that they go
Beyond appointed shores, their bounds
Throughout the years to know?

"And was it you who gave command
That morn should warmly break?
That dawn should know its place and from
The earth the wicked shake?

"And where does light, then, find its place,
And where does darkness dwell?
And have you seen the shades of death
Or viewed the gates of hell?

"Whose womb contains the wintry ice
And who to frost gives birth?
You know these things, of course, for you
Have long dwelt on the earth!

"And by you do the Pleiades
Their brightness find reduced?
And is it at your deft command
Orion's cords are loosed?

"Consider, Job, what you will say,
Just what your words will be,
Would you accuse your God this way?
Would you contend with me?"

Now, well had Job fair answers sought
As God examined him,
But finding none, for none there were,
His countenance was grim.

"Most surely I have spoken, Lord,
Of things I did not know,
For all your plan will be fulfilled
In heav'n and earth below.

"My ears have long been open to
All that I've heard of you,
But now, beholding with my eyes,
With clear, unhindered view,

"Such grand and glorious majesty,
This vision you have sent,
Despising all I am, I now
In dust and ash repent."

Will Not the Judge
of All the Earth Do Right?

(GE 18:16–33)

God told Abraham he was on his way to destroy Sodom. Mindful that his nephew, Lot, and his family lived there, Abraham prays that God will spare the town if fifty, then forty, and so on until finally ten righteous people are found there. Abraham likely thought that Lot, his wife, their three daughters and their daughters' fiancés could be counted righteous, and hoped there were at least two others in the town who lived righteous lives. His prayer follows a brief lead-in.

The men rose up to leave and looked
Toward Sodom 'cross the arid plain,
And by their side walked Abraham,
His people's custom to maintain.

The Lord remained before him there,
And asked if some account were due.
"Shall it be hid from Abraham,
The thing I am about to do?

"For Abraham will soon become
A mighty nation, great and strong.
All peoples will be blessed through him,
And tribute bring in word and song.

"For I have chosen him that he,
In years that follow, may direct
His children and his ample house
In all my ways, true and correct,

"And foll'wing what is just and right,
I will to Abraham at last,
Fulfill my promise made to him
In Haran, many years now past."

The Lord then said to him, "I've heard
The cry 'gainst Sodom in the plain,
Gomorrah, too, has taken part
In all their sins, both vile and vain.

"For this I go to see just what
They've done, and fairly judge their deeds.
And thus discerning, I will know
If any man my law yet heeds."

The men then turned toward Sodom way,
But Abraham remained and stood
Before the Lord, and asked, "Will you
Destroy with evil men the good?

"If fifty righteous men are found,
Will you remove the wicked place,
Not sparing all for their kind sake,
Nor for their honor leave a trace?

"Far be it, Lord, from you this thing
To do before all mankind now,
The righteous with the evil slay,
And thus this travesty allow.

"Will not the Judge of all do right?
Discernment will he fail to make,
'Tween righteous and the wicked man,
And thus the pure of soul forsake?"

"If fifty righteous people there
I find," God said, "within the walls,
I'll spare the place nor suffer that
This final tragedy befalls."

And Abraham once more replied,
"Such boldness I till now have claimed,
Though I am naught but dust and ash.
This plea I make while bowed and shamed:

"If five are lacking mongst them all,
Will you destroy upon the ground,
Both man and woman, beast and home
That in its confines may be found?"

"The city will remain," God said,
"If lacking five of righteous life."
"And what of forty?" was then asked,
"If youth or elder, man or wife?"

"If forty are revealed," God said,
"I'll spare the place from tragedy."
"Now let me speak this word again,
And be not angry with my plea.

"For thirty?" Abraham pursued.
And God vowed kindness offered them.
"Now let my daring not offend,
Will twenty your great anger stem?"

"Yea, e'en for twenty I will save
The town and its environs well."
"Once more your servant deigns to speak
This plea to make and dread to quell:

"And what, O Lord, if ten are found,
Though well you search both high and low?"
"For ten my mercy I'll extend,
And my deserving wrath forgo."

The Lord then left and Abraham,
Returning, soon was homeward bound.
He fairly danced a jig, he was
So confident they would be found.

Jabez – "Enlarge My Territory!"

(1 Ch 4:9, 10)

These two verses are the only account of the man named Jabez. Perhaps God answered his prayer in so noteworthy a way that his vow became well known among Jewish historians, thus its inclusion here. It has been observed that he asked for a life "free from pain." His mother had said, "I gave birth to him in pain."

A man of honored traits and life,
Was Jabez named for this,
His mother gave him birth and said,
"What pain instead of bliss!"

A day arrived when Jabez cried
To Israel's God above,
"That you, oh Lord, would bless me now
In kindness and in love,

"Enlarging my domain and all
Possessions that are mine,
Your hand upon me, keeping from
All harm one may define.

"For thus will I be free from pain,
If you grant my request."
God granted what he asked; he was
Mongst all his brothers, best.

· James Vasquez ·

Water from the Rock

(Ex 17:1-7)

"What am I to do with these people?" Moses cries to the Lord after they accuse him of leading them into the desert only to "make us and our children and livestock die of thirst." God instructs him to walk ahead, with elders, and "strike the rock," where the Lord would be standing by.

The Desert of Sin they had left,
A bleak barren wasteland behind.
Before them good fortune they hoped,
By fate or God's blessing they'd find.

But when they encamped, to dismay,
No water was found any place.
Most angry as death hovered near,
To Moses they said to his face,

"You promised deliv'rance for all,
If foll'wing wherever you led,
Now give us sweet water to drink,
Or soon all our tribe will be dead."

"Your anger with me is misplaced.
For putting the Lord to the test,
You'll not his great blessing receive,
Nor enter the land of true rest."

But still did each man suffer thirst,
'Gainst Moses they spoke, then, this word:
"You brought us from Egypt's sere land,
And hopes for full rescue you stirred.

"It seems now that all was for this:
In wastelands to end all our lives,
Our children's as well as our own,
Where plant nor small animal thrives."

Then Moses cried out to the Lord,
"Now what shall I do with this crowd?
They're ready to stone me but you,
Their safety and sustenance vowed."

The Lord answered faithf'ly his prayer.
"Now walk on ahead of them all,
And with you some elders as well,
Such fate to most quickly forestall,

"The staff well in hand that you used
To strike Egypt's river and pride,
And by the rock there will I stand,
At Horeb where I will provide.

"For as you strike well with the rod,
Sweet water from rock will gush out,
To satisfy Israel's great thirst,
And end this most perilous drought."

In sight of the people then he,
This Moses, did all he was told.
And "testing" and "quarreling" 'twas called,
Though God gave them better than gold.

Moses Atop Sinai

(Ex 32:9-14, 30-34; Dt 9:25-29)

In the first of these three passages, God speaks to Moses after seeing his people worshiping a golden calf they fashioned at the foot of Mt Sinai. Then he speaks to Moses on the mountain, promising to make of him, but not Israel, a great nation. Moses reminds God of his promises to his people, and tells him that such rejection would be mocked by the Egyptians.

In the second passage, Moses has seen the calf and reveling of Israel as the people danced around the idol, and has taken vengeance on many of them. Returning to Mt Sinai he prays for their atonement, telling God that if he cannot forgive his people, "then blot me out of the book you have written." God relents but promises future punishment for his people.

The third passage takes place about forty years later as Israel is poised to enter the promised land. Moses reminds them how he had prayed for them.

(Ex 32:9-14)
Then Moses heard the Lord's firm word:
"My people's sin I've seen," he said,
"A stiff-necked people, one and all,
Now I will make of you, instead,

"A nation great and strong, but first,
Because my righteous anger burns,
Their end I'll bring. 'Tis for their sins
My wrath for satisfaction yearns."

Then Moses sought the favor of
The Lord his God, some grace to win.
"Let not your anger burn against
Your people for their treach'rous sin,

"Whom out from Egypt's brutal lair,
You led by your almighty arm,
That in a land of promise they
Might serve you and be kept from harm.

"For why should it be said of you,
In Egypt's tongue with boundless mirth,
'For ill intent he brought them out
To kill and wipe them from the earth'?

"Now from this anger fierce relent,
Let no disaster come to them,
Your people, born of Abraham,
And Isaac, Israel, sons of Shem.

"By your own self to them you swore,
'Of your descendants I will make
As many as the stars above.
My vow to them I'll not forsake.

"'The land I promised will be theirs,
Their legacy throughout all time.
With milk and honey flowing and
The sun above in pleasant clime.'"

The Lord relented, then, from all
To Jacob's sons he thought to do.
He brought no great disaster on
His people, nor his grace withdrew.

(Ex 32:30-34)
And Moses went to face once more,
The Lord against whom Israel sinned.
"The people's sin is great," he said,
"'Gainst you this vice undisciplined,

"For gods of gold they've made themselves,
But now, I plead, forgive their sin.
If not, then blot me from your book
Where final judgment will begin."

To Moses then the Lord replied,
"Who sins against me I will blot
From out my searching book of life,
And judge with justice, as I ought.

"Now go, lead Israel to the place
I spoke of on dark Sinai's peak.
Before you will my angel go,
To you my statutes he will speak.

"And yet the day will come for me
To punish Israel for their deeds,
And surely will I lay the rod
For perfidy their action breeds."

(Dt 9:25-29)
Those forty days and nights I lay,
Full prostrate there before the Lord,
For your destruction he would seek,
Nor grace nor mercy would accord.

"O Sovereign Lord," I said, "hold back
Your wrath; do not destroy this day
Your people, your inheritance,
For whom, my face in dust, I pray.

"By your great power you redeemed,
And with a mighty hand brought out
From Egypt's land, their fathers who
Your goodness hailed with praise and shout.

"Remember now your servants whom
You raised that they might serve you well,
Great Abraham and Isaac, son,
And Jacob, with whom you would dwell.

"In stubbornness this people live,
But overlook their bent to sin.
In wrath remember mercy and
Their weak and tired hearts within.

"If not, 'twill surely then be said,
Mongst those whence you have led us out,
'The Lord with weakened hand could not
To promised land safeguard, no doubt.

"'He led them out because in truth,
He hated them, and wished to deal
One final blow to end their lives,
Their bones in wastelands to conceal.'

"And yet your people they remain,
Your legacy this very day,
Delivered by your outstretched arm,
Though oft they sin and disobey."

Gideon – The Least Am I

(JDG 6-8)

The text says God sent and angel but as Gideon answers him it is God who speaks. The Israelites have been severely oppressed for seven years by the Midianites, who drive them to seek shelter in mountain clefts, caves and strongholds. They destroy the Israelite crops and livestock. When finally totally impoverished, the Israelites cry out to the Lord for help.

And now I tell you of a man
So filled with doubts and fears,
You'll wonder how it came to be,
And scarce believe your ears,

To hear of how he triumphed and
One day led Israel's men
Against the Midianite army and
To freedom once again.

Yes, Gideon tested God betimes,
To put it kindly and
When once he heard the angel's voice
Resisted each command.

Just how, you ask, could such a man
This victory bring about
Against oppressive Midianites,
And not just win but rout?

Therein my tale consists, dear friend,
Which I'm about to tell,
And set in order how it was
That Gideon fought so well.

For years the Israelites were crushed
In all the land for they
Had chosen to ignore God's law
Nor followed in his way.

And when to God they cried aloud
In heav'n their plea was heard,
An angel then he sent who spoke
This most unusual word:

"The Lord is with you, Gideon,
Your courage is well known,
A mighty warrior are you now
As all your people groan."

And Gideon first then showed his doubts
As in reply he said,
"Then where his wonders as of old
And why such pain instead?

"Please tell me, sir, does it not seem
Our God has left us now,
And though from Egypt he redeemed
He then forgot his vow?"

But God then said he was to go
And from th' oppressor's hand
Deliver Israel and restore
Her fortunes in the land.

And then this feeble answer came:
"The least am I among
My family, which in all our tribe
Is least acclaimed and sung."

"Am I not sending you," God said,
"That you may, hip and thigh,
Smite mightily the Midianites
From plain to heaven high?"

"Now give a sign," the answer was,
"That I may surely know
'Tis you, none else, who speak these words
To whom this charge I owe."

And Gideon quickly offered up
Unleavened bread and meat,
Which, touched by angel's staff was then
Consumed in blazing heat.

An altar then he built to God
And named, The Lord is Peace,
Though in the land the foe still reigned
And war was yet to cease.

· JAMES VASQUEZ ·

Now when the enemy amassed
Its arms and every son,
The Spirit of the Lord came down
To rest on Gideon.

But doubtful still he pleaded then,
If God would save indeed
All Israel by his wavering hand,
Another sign he'd need.

A fleece he now proposed to God
That in the morn quite wet,
He'd find it while the floor around
Would have no dew as yet.

And so it was, he found it just
As he had asked it be,
And promptly, then, he made it known
He had another plea.

"Now let the fleece be dry and 'round
The earth be wet with dew."
And in his kindness God inclined
To grant this favor, too.

Then all his men he gathered and
Prepared to fight a war,
For thirty thousand soldiers came
And then two thousand more.

And now, dear friend, I trust I have
Your questions put to rest
About this doubting man and how
He weathered well the test.

He trusted God though faith was born
A little late, some say,
Yet soon or late what pleases God
Is how one ends the day.

Samson – One Final Time

(Jᴅɢ 16)

Samson had great strength, which by God's choice lay in his uncut hair. By that strength he defeated the oppressive Philistines time after time. He also had great weakness, which was evident in his attraction to foreign women. When he met Delilah his fate was determined. Finally revealing to her the secret of his strength, his hair was cut as he lay asleep on her lap and he was overcome and made a slave when hidden Philistines pounced on him and put out his eyes. Slowly his hair grew out again. At a celebration in their temple, and standing between the two pillars that supported the edifice, he prayed and asked God for one last show of strength.

And as I stand 'tween pillars here,
The victory they've won
Has brought them all together and
Their chanting has begun:

"Let Samson here perform for us
Some lively caper now,
As we to Dagon lift our voice
And in his presence bow.

"Our god this enemy has quelled
Who ravaged all our land,
Who countless sons has cruelly slain
By his once mighty hand."

In Dagon's temple now I turn
And make this soft appeal,
That with my hands outstretched I might
Those mighty pillars feel.

And now I pray, "O Sovereign Lord,
Remember me this day,
And grant that for my eyes I might
Most vengefully repay.

"One final time renew my strength,
I earnestly now cry,
For with these Philistines I am
Content, O Lord, to die!"

My helpless plea is borne aloft,
God hears and *does* approve,
And now a mighty rumbling comes
As I those pillars move.

· JAMES VASQUEZ ·

Hannah – "It Is Not By Strength"

(1 Sᴀ 1, 2)

In her first prayer Hannah asked for a son. Year after year she prayed, but "the Lord had closed her womb." In bitterness of soul and midst much weeping she continued to pray. She vowed that if God granted her a son, she would "give him to the Lord for all the days of his life." God granted her request. In this prayer Hannah praises God, even though addressing him directly only once, and extols his sovereignty over all men, for he punishes the wicked and raises the poor and needy, seating them "with princes."

A prayer from deep within her soul
Ascended to the throne,
Where God in majesty prevailed,
In hopes that he would own

This forlorn woman's ardent plea
That she might bear a son,
And of her scornful barrenness
And ridicule be done.

"O Lord Almighty, look upon
Your lowly servant here.
Behold my wretched misery,
Each bitter, flowing tear.

"Forget me not, my earnest plea
Ascends to you on high,
And give to me a son lest I,
In abject sorrow die.

"To you shall he be given, Lord,
To serve you all his days.
No razor will come near his head
As he attends your ways."

Can God his children e'er deny,
Does he in truth have choice,
Entreated thus so helplessly
When by the faintest voice?

And weaned, young Samuel took his place
And spent his youthful days
Within the temple, thence to bear
The God of Israel praise.

And Hannah, once her prayer appeased,
Broke forth in joyful song,
Which kindles still in grateful hearts
And shall for ages long.

"My heart rejoices in the Lord,
My horn is lifted high,
And o'er the enemy I boast
Whose fateful end is nigh.

· JAMES VASQUEZ ·

"There is no other Holy One,
No Rock who can compare
With you, O Lord, who stand alone
And heav'n's bright raiment wear.

"Let not proud men with loosened tongues
Now arrogantly prate,
For he who knows all things one day
Will justify their fate.

"The warriors' bows has he destroyed,
But those who stumbled find
With strength renewed, God lifted them
And to their needs inclined.

"And those who were of stomach full
And by their palates led,
Now sell themselves despondently
And labor for their bread.

"The hungry feel the pangs no more
Of emptiness and thirst,
For God their plight has kindly seen
And all their fate reversed.

"The barren one of children now
No less than sev'n has borne,
But she once ringed by many sons
Alone at last will mourn.

"The Lord is he who death refers,
Who makes alive again,
And whether Sheol or life beyond
He renders the Amen.

"For poverty and wealth alike
Are by his hand bestowed.
The humbled and exalted thus
Are to his preference owed.

"And from the dust the poor are raised,
From ash heaps those in need.
He seats them 'longside princes fair
And those of noble breed.

"The earth's foundations are his own,
On them the world is set.
The feet of all his saints he guards
And stills the wicked yet.

"For not by strength does one prevail.
Whoe'er shall God oppose,
His thund'ring voice at judgment will
Their wanton deeds expose.

"But to the king shall strength be giv'n
In every wanting day.
The horn of God's anointed is
Exalted now and aye."

· JAMES VASQUEZ ·

Who Am I, O Sovereign Lord?

(2 Sam 7:18-29)

During a time of peace not long after he was anointed king, David thought it wasn't right that he lived in a house of cedar while the Lord's house was a tent. God sends the prophet Nathan to tell David that he was not to build a grand temple. His son would build a house for God. "Then King David went in and sat before the Lord:"

And hearing what the prophet said,
Great David sat alone before
The Lord in hopes some words to find,
His praises to outpour.

Now who am I, O Sovereign Lord,
And what the name my family bears,
That this great honor you bestow
Beyond my hopes and prayers?

And failing this to satisfy
All that within your heart is found,
Your promise comes that for all time
My house shall be renowned.

But scarcely can I think this way
You've taken me by kindly hand
Is how, with each and every man,
You deal throughout the land.

And words now falter on my lips
As I some worthy utterance seek,
Of thanks, of praise, acknowledgement,
That all your love bespeak.

By sovereign will and spoken word
You've chosen thus to honor me,
Fulfilling now the promises,
Disclosing your decree.

How great your Name, O Sovereign Lord,
There is no other who compares,
That you alone are God we've known
From sainted, wise forebears.

Your people, Lord, elect as well,
No other nation did you choose,
Redeeming Israel for yourself,
Which pride nor life did lose.

The nations that before us stood
You banished with their gods of stone.
You led us to the promised land
And made its wealth our own!

Forever, Lord, our bounds are set,
From Pisgah's heights to ocean shores.
Our God you have become just as
Forever we are yours.

· JAMES VASQUEZ ·

Now keep, O Lord, your word disclosed
　　To David and his house fore'er,
Your name its due acclaim receive,
　　Its just renown declare.

And men will say, "The mighty God
　　Is he who reigns o'er Israel,"
Of David's house established firm,
　　All peoples then will tell.

Your word, O Lord, to build my house
　　Has loosed this prayer I utter now,
Your promise to bring good to me
　　I find a faithful vow.

Be pleased to bless this house of mine
　　Bestowing good and length of years,
And blest, we shall your praises sing
　　Through times of joy or tears.

Solomon Asks For Wisdom

(1 Kɪ 3:5-15)

Solomon's great temple was not yet built and his people were offering sacrifices on the "high places." Solomon loved the Lord and walked in his statutes, though he also offered sacrifices on the high places. In a dream God asked him what he wanted God to give him. Solomon's answer: "I am only a little child and do not know how to carry out my duties . . . (G)ive your servant a discerning heart to govern your people and distinguish between right and wrong."

'Twas in a dream the Lord appeared
To Solomon when night was deep,
In Gibeon where he held court,
And he lay fast asleep.

"Now ask whatever I shall give,
It shall be yours assuredly."
And Solomon gave thought at once,
Then answered hurriedly:

"Great kindness to your servant, Lord,
To David did you show when king,
For he walked faithf'ly in your ways,
And would your praises sing.

"His heart was wholly like your own,
And ever upright in your eyes.
Today, your kindness yet remains,
As fortune testifies.

· JAMES VASQUEZ ·

"This very day throughout the land,
His son now reigns upon the throne,
For you have made your servant king,
To Israel's borders known.

"Yet, I am but a child today,
Untaught in ways to govern well,
Mongst chosen people whose vast sum
I cannot know or tell.

"Grant to your servant, then, a heart,
That Israel he may rule aright,
And wisdom to perceive 'tween wrong
And just both day and night.

"For who is able, Lord, this throng,
This mighty tribe to justly rule?
And lacking wisdom all will think
That I am but a fool."

The Lord was pleased that Solomon
Asked not for silver or for gold,
Nor for the death of enemies,
Nor life advanced and old.

And thus he said, "Since you have asked
Above all else for this of me,
Discernment and just ways that yours
A righteous reign may be,

"What you have asked I will bestow,
A heart most wise, discerning and
Like you no man alive will be,
Or was in all the land.

"And what you've not implored as well,
I give to you that you may own,
Such riches and true honor that
Mongst kings you'll stand alone.

"And if you walk in all my ways,
Obey my statutes and commands,
As David did who worshiped me
And lifted holy hands,

"Then will I make quite full your years,
For Israel's needs you have revered."
And Solomon awoke to find
In dreams God had appeared.

Then straightway to Jerus'lem he
Returned and stood before the ark,
Which signified the cov'nant made
On Sinai, dread and dark.

And sacrifices to his God
He offered up with fire and smoke,
Then gave a feast for all his court,
And told them what God spoke.

Solomon Dedicates the Temple

(1 Ki 8:22-53)

Solomon's glorious temple had been built and, surrounded by the priests and Levites and the entire assembly of Israel, the ark of the covenant was taken from the Tent of Meeting and placed inside the temple, within the Most Holy Place. It contained only the two stone tablets with the inscription of the Ten Commandments, made by Moses after he destroyed the first two tablets. The ark was placed beneath the wings of the two cherubim, made of hammered gold.

> *The temple stood before the throng*
> *Assembled there around,*
> *Most glorious in its majesty,*
> *On marbled, holy ground.*
>
> *Its glist'ning columns reaching up*
> *As if to pierce the sky,*
> *That he who heav'n and earth brought forth*
> *Might ever more be nigh.*
>
> *With arms outstretched in prayerful pose,*
> *In honored, royal dress,*
> *Great Solomon his God implored*
> *To e'er his people bless.*

· James Vasquez ·

O God who reigns in majesty
In lustrous heights above,
Who ever faithful, keeps his oath,
His covenant of love,

O Israel's God none can compare
Among the gods men know,
In might or wisdom, honor, power
In heav'n or earth below.

Your promise, Lord, is kept today
To all your people here,
For David's son now wears the crown
And rules without a peer.

Your mouth sent forth the word which then
Your mighty hand fulfilled,
And now your servants have complied
With all that you have willed.

This temple have I built, O Lord,
A house forever yours,
That in your splendrous essence you
Might dwell within its doors.

But will indeed our God reside
In structures man has made?
The heav'ns themselves will disappoint
Though broadly yet arrayed.

· JAMES VASQUEZ ·

35

But hear, O Lord, your servant's plea
When toward this house he prays,
And grant him mercy for his sins
On this and all his days.

And when your people lift their voice
Wherever they may live,
And toward this house direct their prayer,
Then hear, Lord, and forgive.

For you have said your Name shall be
Where now this temple stands,
To hear your peoples' prayers as they
Lift upward holy hands.

And judge between your servants, Lord,
Who by this altar swear,
And let the innocent be known,
The guilty ones declare.

And when your people, carried off
Afar to foreign lands,
Because with hardened hearts they turned,
Forgetting your commands,

Shall thence in captor's field once more
Confess your holy Name,
And supplication make to you,
Acknowledging their shame,

Then hear afar as from this place
And bring them to this land,
Which to their fathers you bequeathed
With strong, exalted hand.

When heavens hold the rain within
Each laden, darksome cloud,
For sin among your people has
A blighting curse allowed,

Then hearing as they turn again
Toward this great house of prayer,
Restore to them the rains of yore,
Removing their despair.

And when the land is buffeted
By famine, plague or drought,
Or armies have assailed our towns
And ring them all about,

Whatever, Lord, the curse may be,
When Israel turns again,
Then hear, forgive and bless for you
Know well the hearts of men.

And deal with each according to
His deeds before you plain,
That men may fear you as they ought
And in the land remain.

· JAMES VASQUEZ ·

The foreigner will hear and come
Because of your great Name,
And 'fore this temple standing will
Your mighty works acclaim.

And may his prayer ascend to you
That all men where he dwells
May fear your Name as he returns,
And of your glory tells.

Hear now, O Lord, your people's call
In heaven high above,
For Israel have you singled out
Mongst nations in your love.

And through your servant Moses you
With potent, holy hand,
Have made a people for yourself
And called from Egypt's land.

Now rise, great God, and take your place
As song and sacred hymn
Intone your praises o'er the ark
And wingéd cherubim.

May all your priests forever in
Salvation's glad attire
With righteous hearts their offering make,
Their virtue ne'er expire.

And may your people, highly blessed
For all your goodness known,
Throughout their days rejoice as they
Your rich provision own.

And in his more exalted days
And days of failure too,
Remember your anointed one,
Requiting not his due,

For to his father David you
The promise now bestow,
That those who o'er his kingdom rule
Your love would ever know.

The Things I Ask of Thee

(Pr 30:7-9)

The prayer is attributed to Agur, son of Jakeh. The writer took eleven lines in the first verses of the chapter to exalt the Lord for his greatness and might in creation. In appropriate humility he then writes this prayer, asking for freedom from falsehood and for not too much or little in life.

Remove, O Lord, keep from my life,
This do I ask of thee,
Dishonesty and low pretense,
Untainted let me be,

Before thine eyes that see all things
And search and search again,
For hearts that scorn duplicity
To find among all men.

For how shall I in falsehood live
And then before thee stand,
When truth alone may dwell with thee
And is thy clear command?

And well I've learned and have no doubt
In lies there is no gain.
They cannot cover what we've done
As found our brother Cain.

And yet before their power, Lord,
Our bent is infamous.
Our very helplessness thus pleads
Thou wilt deliver us.

And then, O Lord, I ask as well
Thou wilt provide for me,
That I should have just what I need
And from all greed be free.

That I may of those foods partake
Which all my body's need
Without excess of garnishment,
Sufficiently will feed.

And give me not so gen'rously
The riches men may seek,
For when the power of wealth is mine
In truth, Lord, I am weak.

And in that day I will forget
Whence wealth has been bestowed,
And then deny the very God
To whom all things are owed.

But do not either, Lord, I ask,
A poor man make of me,
For then in weakness will I make
Of faith a parody.

· JAMES VASQUEZ ·

I fear I will put forth my hand
To take what is not mine,
To ease the burden of my needs,
To clothe me, or to dine.

For I would not profane thy name
For any cause whate'er,
No matter what temptations lurk
Or call me to their snare.

Nor rich nor poor then, is my plea,
For I in weakness dwell,
And thus my soul in peace shall rest
And all they glories tell.

Elijah and the Widow's Son

(1 Kɪ 17)

For a while things went well for Elijah. A widow had taken him in and fed him
and her son (with help from God, who provided an unending supply of flour and
oil). But then the boy died and the woman blamed Elijah. "What do you have
against me, man of God? Did you come to remind me of my sin and kill my son?"
Elijah took the boy in his arms, carried him to his upper room, and prayed.

But fate in its unfathomed ways
Had not yet dealt its final blow,
Forever seeking one on whom
    Its scourges to bestow.

An illness came upon her son,
And though she gave him utmost care,
His circumstance but worsened till
    His life it did not spare.

He died and then the widow turned
On poor Elijah for his death.
"And is it for my sin you've come
    To rob my son of breath?"

He took the boy within his arms
And to his upper room withdrew.
He placed the boy upon his bed,
    One gracious thing to do.

He knew not of the woman's sin
But that his prayer was ever heard
By Israel's God above who then,
His healing hand bestirred.

"Oh, Lord, now why such tragedy
Upon this lowly widow brought?
And why this needless, wrenching death
Upon her son you've wrought?"

His earnest cry was heard throughout
The widow's home with mourners filled.
He stretched himself upon the boy,
Of life and breath yet stilled.

Once more a cry was heard within
The prophet's barren, upper den.
"Oh, Lord my God, now raise the boy
And grant him life again!"

And he whose ear is e'er inclined
To every servant's helpless voice
Reached forth his strong, majestic arm,
And healed by sovereign choice.

"Behold!" the prophet said, "Your son
Within my arms—alive and well!
Let mourning cease and praise to God
Be what your lips now tell."

The woman rushed to hold her son,
Awaiting her with winsome smile
And brightly shining, boyish eyes
That ever would beguile.

"I know you are a man of God
And speak the truth, by this," she said.
"For by his might and goodness is
My son raised from the dead."

Elijah and the Prophets of Baal

(1 Kɪ 18)

At the word of Elijah, King Ahab gathered four hundred and fifty prophets of Baal for a contest to see whose was the true God. Elijah was confident his was the true God, even saying to the people of Israel that if Baal proved to be God they should follow him. For hours Baal's prophets offered incantations, danced and even shed their blood in their attempts to induce Baal to show himself. Finally, Elijah prepared his own altar and sacrificed a bull, drenching it all with water. Then he prayed.

And forward then I stepped and prayed,
"O God of Abraham,
Of Isaac and of Israel,
The Lord, the great I AM,

"Now let your people understand
That you alone are God,
And turn their hearts again to you,
For them to know and laud.

"These things I've done at your command
That they may know that I
Am but your faithful servant and
On you alone rely."

And hardly had I finished when
From high above there came
A fire reaching to the earth,
A ruinous, heav'n-sent flame.

In but a moment it consumed
The sacrifice and wood,
Nor e'en the water in the trench
Its blazing heat withstood.

The stones were melted, then were naught,
The soil around destroyed,
And everything the fire touched
Was of all life devoid.

The people saw and prostrate fell.
They knew beyond a doubt
Just who was God and who was not,
And they began to shout,

"The Lord is God! The Lord is God!"
And then this word I gave,
That Baal's prophets should be seized
With none to help or save.

And off to Kishon's Valley were
They taken at my word,
And there the people slaughtered them
And Israel's sin—deferred.

Hezekiah – "You Alone Are God"

(2 Kɪ 19:14-20, 32-34; Is 37:14-21, 33-35)

King Hezekiah received a letter from Sennacherib, the Assyrian general whose troops were ravaging nation after nation. In pointed detail Sennacherib reminds Hezekiah that no nation had withstood the onslaught of the Assyrian army and says Hezekiah's God will not be able to defend Jerusalem, just as the gods of Gozan, Haran, Rezeph and Eden had not defended their people. After reading the letter, Hezekiah went to the temple of the Lord, spread the letter out before the Lord, and prayed.

The letter came and was reviewed,
King Hezekiah read it well.
Then quickly to the temple went,
Its dire content there to tell.

He spread it plain before the Lord,
And eyes uplifted, prayed to him,
"O Lord and Israel's God enthroned
Between exalted cherubim,

"Alone o'er kingdoms everywhere,
You reign supreme, if land or sea,
For you have made both heav'n and earth.
Give ear, O Lord, and hear my plea.

"With eyes ope'd wide, now see, O Lord,
With ears attuned this message hear.
Sennacherib insults your name,
While lacking forethought and all fear.

"Assyrian kings in every place
To many nations have laid waste.
They've taken lands and idols smashed,
And thus destroyed what was embraced.

"For all were made by craftsmen's hands,
But gods of falsehood now and e'er,
Of wood and stone and crudely carved,
Of consequence most fully bare.

"Deliver us, our God, from his
Swift horses, spear and brutal rod,
And kingdoms all will be assured
That you, O Lord, alone are God."

Isaiah, prophet, seer, then sent
To Hezekiah in his woe,
This message: "I have heard your prayer
For my deliv'rance from the foe.

"Assyria's king will build no ramp
Against this city's humble wall.
He'll shoot no arrow, bear no shield,
Or cause its ramparts here to fall.

"For whence he came he shall return,
And I, the Lord, for David's sake,
Will save this place from foreign hands,
And all my righteous zeal awake."

· JAMES VASQUEZ ·

A Prayer of Asa

(2 Ch 14:9-13)

Asa was a good king, walking in the Lord's ways and doing much good for his people. His kingdom enjoyed peace until a "vast army" came out from the land of Cush, led by Zerah. Though Asa's army itself numbered over half a million armed men, the Cushite army was significantly larger. The armies took up battle positions in a valley, and Asa prayed.

Then Zerah, chief of Cushites, marched
'Gainst Asa and his men ahead,
He led an army vast, and hoped
King Asa's men to leave quite dead.

Three hundred chariots went before
And finally reached Maresha, where
Brave Asa and his forces camped.
The armies would do battle there.

Then to the Lord his God he called,
This Asa, king and man of war,
"No power like yours is found to help
The powerless now or yet before,

"And 'gainst the mighty have we come,
This day to battle in your name.
Now help us, Lord, for we rely
On you, of known repute and fame.

"This vast and awesome army that
Before us wields both horse and spear,
We cannot by our strength resist,
While fears increase as it draws near.

"But you, our God beyond compare,
Reserve great might and wisdom still.
Let not these men prevail against
Your name, your honor or your will."

The Lord then struck the Cushites down
In sight of Asa and his men,
Who rose, pursuing, till the foe
Was beaten 'cross both hill and glen.

And Asa's men much booty took
From villages around the site.
The fear of God upon them came,
Who saw their army put to flight.

Isaiah's Vision – "Whom Shall I Send?"

(Isa 6)

Isaiah, a priest in Judah, lived in the eighth century, B.C. One day he entered the temple and had this incomparable vision, resulting in a commission from God. When writing of this experience later he attests its historical veracity by citing the very year the vision came to him, "the year that King Uzziah died," (about 740 B.C.).

The year Uzziah died I saw
Exalted on a throne,
The Lord uplifted and his train
Did all the temple own.

And seraphs hovered round the Lord
And filled the temple, too.
With wings they covered face and feet,
With twain they swiftly flew.

They called to one another as
Their orbed flights they pursued,
A hallowed, singular refrain,
Unceasingly renewed.

"Now holy, holy, holy is
The Lord whose glory fills
From end to end the earth, its seas,
Its mountains and its hills."

And at their voice the thresholds shook
The temple to its base,
While door-posts trembled on their stands
And smoke filled all the place.

And in my fright at visions such
As I had never known,
I called aloud most desperately
For all my sin was shown.

Yes, I beheld in that great light
The glory of the Lord,
And brightly it exposed my life
And every sin deplored.

"Oh! Woe to me for I am ruined,
Undone for all my sin.
A man of unclean lips am I
Midst unclean friends and kin.

"My eyes have seen, my ears have heard
And scarce to life I cling,
For I in truth this day beheld
The face of God the King."

· JAMES VASQUEZ ·

But kindly then, a coal was pressed,
Red, glowing from the fire,
Which there upon the altar burned,
Appeasing holy ire,

Upon my lips by seraph sent
From him who sat enthroned,
For he my guilt had now removed
And for my sin atoned.

Then once again, nay, so much more,
The temple shook throughout,
And dumb were tongues of seraphs as
The voice of God rang out.

"Now is there man who for our right
Will go for us today?
And whom will I now find mongst men
To send him on my way?"

"Great God, send me for I am here,"
I hurriedly then said.
I scarce before that glory dared
Another word instead.

"Then go and to my people say,"
The Lord replied to me,
"With eyes to see and ears to hear,
In dullness ever be.

"And hardened shall their hearts remain,
Their eyes and ears e'er sealed.
Lest with an understanding heart
They turn and then are healed."

"How long, O Lord?" I then implored,
And felt for Israel's plight.
"Till cities lie all desolate
And fields are scourged with blight,

"Till houses stand deserted and
To distant lands are sent
My people for their many sins,
To raise their sad lament.

"A tenth yet shall remain at home
To suffer further waste.
Yet as a stump this holy seed
By God will be embraced."

I pondered much on what this meant,
This charge he gave to me,
The devastation, exile, stump,
And what their ends might be.

And from that day I've faltered not
In speaking what I heard,
That Israel might with open ears
Admit his certain word.

· JAMES VASQUEZ ·

Isaiah's Song of Praise

(Isa 26)

*This chapter immediately follows one promising the restoration of God's people,
when the "Sovereign Lord will wipe away the tears from all faces; he will remove
the disgrace of his people from all the earth." Thus, chapter twenty-six is rightly
titled "A Song of Praise." The song is unusual in that it clearly speaks of a
resurrection, as in the phrases, "but your dead will live; their bodies will rise . . .
the earth will give birth to her dead" (verse nineteen). Several oft-quoted verses
are contained in the Song, which, though the writer at times addresses God's
people, he mostly addresses God.*

Within the land of Judah shall
This song of praise be sung by all,
The day our fortunes are restored,
The day our favors we recall.

Our city's walls and ramparts are
By the Almighty 'stablished well.
Salvation he has made them for
His people who in safety dwell.

Now open wide the gates that they,
The righteous, may have entrance here,
The nation that has kept its faith,
That walks before the Lord in fear.

In perfect peace you keep the man
Whose mind is ever fixed on you,
For he has found your spoken word
In all things and all times is true.

Now trust in him th' eternal Rock,
Yea, trust his word for aye.
The Lord, the Lord will speak his word,
And it will be your shield and stay.

He humbles those who dwell on high,
He lays the lofty city low,
For to the ground he levels it
And makes it dust the winds will blow.

The feet of the oppressed will rise
And trample on each remnant there.
The poor will stomp in sheer delight
On ruins, and their transport share.

The Upright One makes smooth the way
The righteous take midst all their days.
Yea, Lord, we wait for you and walk
In wisdom that your law displays.

By night, by day for you I long,
Whose name and great renown are known.
My heart's desire, my spirit's quest,
Naught else will I pursue or own.

When on the earth your judgments come,
The people learn all righteousness,
But those who see and turn from grace,
Continue in their wickedness.

Though found among the righteous they
Continue in their evil chores.
The majesty of him who reigns,
Each one disdains and then deplores.

Your hand, O Lord, is lifted high,
But blind, they see it not nor care.
Now put the wicked men to shame,
Your zeal for all your own declare.

And fire you have reserved for them,
Your enemies of paltry worth.
Oh, let them be consumed, their kind
For e'er removed from off the earth.

You grant to us your peace, O Lord,
And deeds of which we vainly boast
Are done, in truth, by your right hand,
If numbered we would find a host.

And other lords have ruled o'er us
But you alone we honor well.
Expired, they've gone to meet their fate
Where spirits must forever dwell.

· James Vasquez ·

To ruin you have brought them and
All mem'ry of their kind erased.
Such punishment they merited
For wanton mutiny embraced.

Our nation you enlarged, O Lord,
Its borders reach a distant land.
Much glory for yourself you gained
As peoples fell at your command.

They came to you in great distress
When you had chastened them for deeds.
They strained to whisper, say a prayer,
As one in dire misfortune needs.

And as a woman writhes in pain
When bringing forth a child to light,
So we, when in your presence, Lord,
Cried out in anguish for our plight.

For though with child, enduring pain,
To naught but wind did we give birth.
'Twas not the people we brought forth,
Nor your salvation in the earth.

But you, O earth, your dead will rise,
And you who dust's deep vaults now tread,
Wake up with shouts of joy, for earth
Will yet surrender all her dead.

· JAMES VASQUEZ ·

Now go, my people, to your rooms,
Close well each door behind and hide,
Until his wrath has passed you by.
The Lord comes forth, resolved in stride.

He comes from out his dwelling place
To punish men for sins concealed.
The earth will no more hide their blood,
Her slain will finally be revealed.

Jeremiah's Lamentations

(3:55–66; 5:1-22)

Seven times in the first five chapters of this book the author turns to God in prayer. Each time his words are heavy with either self-pity, pity for Israel's condition, remorse for Israel's sins and/or confession. The book is rightly titled, "Lamentations." The first four prayers are quite short, the last three considerably longer. I have chosen prayers from chapters three and five to include here; from chapter three because it represents much in Jeremiah's prayers that are centered on himself; chapter five (a prayer throughout) because of the strong historical detail regarding Israel's deplorable condition.

(3:55-66)
They hunted me as though a bird,
My enemies for no good cause.
Within a pit they threw their stones
My life to give it pause.

Above my head the waters closed
And surely then I thought 'twas o'er.
"Close not your ears, O Lord," I called,
"Nor my weak cry deplore!"

And from the slimy pit's foul depths
You heard my cry for swift relief.
"Fear not," you said as you came near
To end my frenzied grief.

O Lord, you took my case to mind.
You judged me and my life redeemed.
The wrong I suffered you have seen,
That others willed and schemed.

Uphold my cause for it is right.
Their spiteful vengeance you have known.
Their plots against me never cease
Nor insults they intone.

Throughout the day and by each night
They whisper and then mutter long.
Now look! They stand or sit the while
They mock me in their song.

Now pay them, Lord, what they deserve,
For what their hands have meanly done,
And veiling well their hearts, a curse
Decree for every one.

In anger, then, pursue them till
From underneath all heaven's sky
They are destroyed in every place,
And we may watch them die.

(5:1-22)
The things that happened to us, Lord,
Remember now midst our disgrace.
We've lost our rich inheritance,
Our homes no more embrace.

The foreigner has taken all
And we are left as orphans now.
Our mothers mourn as widows and
In vain before you bow.

For water we must pay a price,
Just as for wood they charge a fee.
Pursuers gather at our heels
Wherever we may flee.

Exhausted and without a rest,
To Egypt and Assyria we
Submitted that some bread we'd find
In hopes they'd hear our plea.

Our fathers sinned and are no more,
Their punishment we bear this day,
For slaves now rule throughout the land
With none to end their sway.

We risk our lives for common bread,
The desert sword devours all,
And like an oven is our skin
From fever's dreaded pall.

Our women have been ravished and
Our virgins throughout Judah's towns.
Our princes by their hands hung up
In flowing, regal gowns.

The elders are not shown respect;
At millstones young men toil the day.
'Neath loads of wood we see our boys
Who stagger in the way.

The city gates are empty for
No elder takes his wonted place.
Of music from young men we fail
To hear the faintest trace.

Where once we danced we mourn aloud,
And from each heart our joy is gone.
The crown has fallen from our head
With naught to place thereon.

Now woe to us for we have sinned.
Our saddened hearts are worn and faint.
Our eyes grow dim for all these things
And vain is our complaint.

Mount Zion we but dimly see
For desolate it yet remains,
And jackals prowl o'er ruins there
Where death's foul stench now reigns.

Your throne, O Lord, shall endless be,
Which man in every age reveres.
Then why are we forgotten and
Forsaken all these years?

Restore us to yourself, O Lord,
And then shall we return to you.
Renew us as in days of old
When amity we knew,

Unless 'tis found that beyond hope
You have rejected us for aye,
Your anger such no balm our sin
Will pardon or allay.

· JAMES VASQUEZ ·

Daniel Prays for his Nation

(9:1–19)

After the fall of Babylon to the Persians and Darius took the throne, Daniel was restored to high position, becoming one of three administrators who governed the 120 satraps (provinces) of the kingdom. In the first year of that appointment he learned from the Scriptures, likely the writings of Jeremiah, that the Exile would last a total of seventy years. For this reason he turned to God and prayed for his nation, "in fasting and in sackcloth and ashes."

'Twas in the year Darius reigned,
His first, this Mede, upon the throne.
I learned from Jeremiah's hand,
Once writ in Scripture, long since known,

Jerus'lem's desolation would
Three score and ten of years endure.
For this, in fasting, sackcloth and
In ashes I pursued some cure.

To God I turned in earnest prayer,
Confessing all our sin with tears,
In hopes, most merciful, he'd hear
My plea, to grant and quell my fears.

Thus I confessed to God, my Lord:
"O great and awesome God above,
With those who love you and obey,
You keep your covenant of love,

"Our lives before you are most plain,
For we have sinned and followed wrong.
Rebellious, we have turned away
From your commandments as a throng.

"We listened not to prophets who
In your blest name have spoken well,
To kings and princes, fathers and
To all who in our nation dwell.

"For you are righteous, Lord, though we
This day are covered with but shame,
Within the land or nations far,
Where'er we're known by your great Name.

"Unfaithfulness has marked our ways
In all lands, scattered by your hand.
Our kings, our princes, every man
Has fully turned from your command.

"And though we've fallen in such sin,
The Lord our God is merciful,
Forgiving our rebellious ways,
Displaying mercy plentiful.

"All Israel stands before you, Lord,
Transgressions are our daily fare.
Your law, your spoken word dismissed,
As we all faithfulness forswear.

"The curses, thus, and judgments vowed,
Long written in great Moses' Law,
Are poured upon us for our sins,
For we at Sinai glory saw.

"And by disaster you fulfilled
The word once spoken years long past,
Against our rulers, us as well,
For sins our people had amassed.

"Yea, nothing done 'neath heaven high,
Has yet compared with what occurred
To our Jerus'lem, barren waste,
And all the world this day has heard.

"Yet we have not God's favor sought,
'Spite this disaster where we dwell.
Nor all our sins forsaken, nor
Your truths attended close and well.

"The Lord did not delay his wrath,
For he is righteous in all things.
He judges all who sin at will
Mongst man and woman, prince and kings.

"And now, O Lord our God, who from
The fires of Egypt led us out,
And who, with mighty hand, a name
Most glorious thus has brought about,

"Which to this day unchanged endures,
In keeping with each righteous act,
Turn from your anger and your wrath,
Remember mercy and your pact.

"For those around us look with scorn
Upon your city, holy hill,
For sins we have committed and
For guilt that weighs upon us still.

"Now hear your servant's voice, O Lord,
Petitions that I bring today.
For your blest sake, O Lord, now see
Most kindly where we come to pray.

"Your sanctuary is a waste.
Give ear, O God, and know our shame.
Now see the desolation wrought
Within the place that bears your Name.

"We ask these favors of you, Lord,
Not for a righteousness we own,
But for your mercy, great and true,
That through the ages has been known.

"O listen, Lord, and then forgive!
And act for your most blessed sake.
Do not delay, your city and
Its people in your Name partake."

Ezra – "With Outstretched Hands"

(Ezr 9:5-15)

Ezra the priest and teacher of the Law lived about one hundred years after the first Jews returned from exile in Babylon. His mission was to help his people settle in the land and follow the Law of God. To his great dismay, he learned the people had mingled with the Canaanites and several other non-Jewish peoples in the land, giving their sons and daughters to them in marriage. On hearing this he tore his tunic, pulled hair from his head and beard and "sat down appalled." At the evening sacrifice he fell on his knees with hands spread out to the Lord and prayed.

'Twas at the evening sacrifice
I quit my deep humility,
My tunic torn, as well my cloak,
To lift to God my earnest plea.

Upon my knees, with outstretched hands
In hopes he might incline his ear,
I prayed, that by good fortune he
Would stoop and my entreaty hear.

"To lift my face to you, O God,
I am disgraced, ashamed to tell,
For higher than our heads our sins
Have mounted up, our guilt as well.

· JAMES VASQUEZ ·

71

"Yea, to the highest heav'n they're found.
In truth, e'er since our father's day,
The greatness of our guilt was known,
That sacrifice could not allay.

"Our kings, our priests, ourselves have known
The foe's cruel sword upon us hard,
Captivity and pillage are
Our lot, in lowly disregard.

"For thus have foreign kings displayed
Contempt for all your people here.
Their armies ravaged all the land,
Nor pity knew in any year.

"But now by your most gracious act,
If only for a moment, Lord,
A remnant you have spared at last,
Relieving us of strife and sword.

"Within your sanctuary are
We found, a safe and sheltered place.
And thus has light come to our eyes,
Relief from bondage we embrace.

"Our God has not deserted us
Though slaves in bondage yet we are,
For kindness has he shown us in
The eyes of Persian kings afar.

"New life he's giv'n that we may build
The house of God with brick and stone,
And from the ruins it will rise,
As he protects us from his throne.

"But what, O God, are we to say?
For all that in our midst occurred
When we dismissed your holy law,
The prophets spoke this fateful word:

"'The land before you is unclean,
Corrupted in extreme degree.
Its practices from end to end,
Have filled it with impurity.

"'Give not your daughters, thus, to them,
Nor may you take their sons as yours.
No treaty may you seek with them,
Nor friendship, which my soul deplores.

"'And thus, forsaking baneful ties,
In promised land you'll eat good things,
Great strength you'll know and leave your sons,
A legacy fit well for kings.'

"Our evil deeds and guilt mount up,
And bring upon our people, Lord,
This great misfortune in our lives,
With loss of land and blood-soaked sword.

· JAMES VASQUEZ ·

73

"Yet you, our God, have brought to us
Less punishment than sins deserve,
And granted us this remnant that
Your will we worthily may serve.

"But shall we break your law again
And marry those who live each day,
Midst practices corrupt and vile,
That vex your soul in every way?

"Would you not, then, such anger know
That our destruction, close at hand,
Would visit us and leave no man
Or yet survivor in the land?

"O God of Israel and our Lord,
Most righteous in your judgments made,
Now look upon this remnant here,
Whose sins of shameful guilt persuade,

"For them not one of us may stand
Within your presence or draw near.
Show mercy, Lord, and grant to us
That you alone our hearts will fear."

Nehemiah's Prayers

In chapters one, two, four, five, six and thirteen of the book named for him,
Nehemiah lifts his voice and prays to God. In the first six chapters Nehemiah
is directing the construction of Jerusalem's walls, a critical need if the city is to
have protection from enemies. He faced resistance and threats constantly while
involved in this task that was approved by King Artaxerxes I, a Persian king
who reigned over the former Babylonian empire. Each time Nehemiah prays it
is in response to some immediate need, or to ask God to remember all the work
he has done for God.

(1:4-11)
Nehemiah was cupbearer to the king in "Susa, the Capital," where Persian
kings had their winter residence. He had just learned of the ruined conditions of
Jerusalem and its walls. So he prays.

And overcome with sadness then,
For days I mourned and wept,
And to my God a prayer I said
While I my fasting kept,

O great and awesome Lord of all,
O God of heav'n above,
Who keeps for those who do his will
His covenant of love,

Now hear your humble servant's prayer
And let your ear attend,
As I my people's sins confess,
Our customs to amend.

· JAMES VASQUEZ ·

75

For I and all my father's house,
In truth, all Israel's kin,
Have turned aside from Moses' law
And chose instead to sin.

And rightly did you scatter us
Among the enemy,
When from your law we turned our face
And acted faithlessly.

But then in kindness you forgave,
And from the nations took
Our people once again as we
Our blasphemies forsook.

Your servants, Lord, whom you restored
Now hopefully await
Within our city's shattered walls
To learn what is their fate.

O hear my voice, most gracious God,
And grant to me I pray,
Success as to this man I go
To make my plea today.

(2:4)

In this verse Nehemiah is in the presence of the king, and troubled. The king detects his sorrow and asks what is wrong. Nehemiah tells him the condition of Jerusalem, and the king asks if he can do anything for Nehemiah.

Now even greater my surprise
When he then said to me,
"What is it that you wish, my son,
And what your humble plea?"

"O grant in this one moment, Lord,
That's come upon me now,
That wisely I may choose my words,
And fearlessly, somehow.

"If I have pleased the king," I said,
"And favor I have found,
Then send me on to Judah where
Your name is quite renowned."

(4:3-6)
Two enemies who bring trouble to the project are Sanballat and Tobiah.

But then Sanballat rose and with
Tobiah at his side,
He mocked the work that we had done
In words both mean and snide.

"And will these Jews in but a day
This city build again?
Will they restore to life its stones,
These hopeless, feeble men?"

Now look upon us, Lord above,
And how we are despised,
And turn their insults on themselves
For what they have devised,

And send them far afield into
Captivity, for they
The builders have insulted and
Your precepts disobey.

May all their goods be plundered well,
And cover not their guilt,
Remove them from Jerusalem
Till all its walls are built.

(5:19)

Nehemiah also had troubles with his own people. They complained about taxes, having to mortgage their fields. Moreover, their daughters were bought as slaves and they had to borrow at usury levels from their own people. Nehemiah chastises the guilty ones and with his own money feeds many at his table.

So one and all they promised to
Give back what they had seized,
And put an end to their demands
That I might be appeased.

Remember all that I have done
For your great people's sake,
And grant that I might fully of
Your favor, Lord, partake.

(6:9)

The walls are finally rebuilt except for the gates. Sanballat and Geshem the Arab send Nehemiah a message, inviting him to meet them "in one of the villages on the plain of Ono." Nehemiah refuses the invitation, sensing that it was a scheme to harm him. A total of four times the two men send the same message to Nehemiah and he refuses each time. And he prays:

The enemy was not yet through,
They then invited me
To leave my city and to meet
With them quite secretly.

But well aware was I of all
The harm they sought to do.
Increase my strength once more, dear God,
And let it be in you.

(6:14)

Nehemiah's enemies Sanballat and Tobiah send Shemaiah to invite him once again to meet with them, this time "in the house of God." Shemaiah feigns he is on Nehemiah's side, suggesting he "close the temple doors" for his safety. Nehemiah refuses and asks God to remember his enemies "for what they have done." This time he includes among his enemies "Noadiah and the rest of the prophets" who had sought to intimidate him. He prays:

Remember now my enemies
For all their wicked part,
Who ceaselessly endeavor to
Intimidate my heart.

Remember Noadiah well,
And other prophets who,
Together planned as best they could,
The harm they longed to do.

(13:14, 22, 29, 30)
Nehemiah prays briefly no less than four times in this chapter. Each time there is a different reason, or context:

(13:14)
Nehemiah had returned to King Artaxerxes for a period and in his absence the temple had been mismanaged in several ways: Tobiah was given a room there, the Levites had not been given their portions, tithes of grain and new wine had not been put in the storerooms. Upon his return Nehemiah corrects this neglect.

For this remember me, O God.
Let not things I have done,
In service to your house be lost,
Look kindly on each one.

(13:22)
Nehemiah learned that the Sabbath was not being kept, for vendors spent the night outside the closed gates, ready to rush into the city early next morning. Nehemiah threatens to "lay hands" on them if they continued. He commands the Levites to purify themselves and to guard the gates.

Remember this, as well, O God.
Show mercy to me now.
According to your steadfast love,
This kindly grant allow.

(13:29)

Men of Judah had married foreign women from several cities and half of their children could not speak the language of Judah. Nehemiah chastises them, invoking the sin of Solomon, who married many foreign women. Then he learns one of the high priest's sons had married a daughter of Sanballat. He "drove him away."

Remember them, O God, for they
Their priestly role defiled,
Its covenant with Levites and
Its holy charge reviled.

(13:30)

Nehemiah accomplished the notable task of purifying the priests and Levites "of everything foreign." He gave them individual tasks and made provisions for contributions of wood and the firstfruits.

Now kindly, Lord, remember me
For all my labors here,
And let your love upon me rest,
Your favor, Lord, be near.

The Levites –
"Stand Up and Praise the Lord"
(Ne 9:5-38)

The walls restored and temple worship once more observed, the people assemble on the twenty-fourth day of the seventh month and for three hours read from the "Book of the Law of the Lord their God," then for three hours they confess their sins and worship the Lord their God. Eight Levites on the temple stairs command the people to stand and praise God.

The Levites then most boldly said,
"Stand up and praise the Lord your God,"
To Israel's people thus they spoke,
And hoped to leave them shamed and awed.

"From everlasting throughout years,
Your name, O Lord, is to be praised.
Our songs will bless your name alone,
Nor to a foreign god be raised.

"You reign as Lord with none beside.
The heav'ns and highest heav'n you made,
The starry host, the earth and all
The seas upon the sand o'erlaid.

"All creatures by your hand exist
And life you give to all things found.
The multitudes above sing loud,
Excepting none, their songs abound.

· James Vasquez ·

"When Abram you called forth from Ur,
You brought him to this fruitful place,
And Abraham you named him then,
To make of him a chosen race.

"His heart you found most faithful and
A covenant you made with him,
That his descendants should increase,
Nor mem'ry of this compact dim.

"Your promises you kept, O Lord,
For you are righteous in all things.
Your praise, unsilenced everywhere
Within all heav'n and earth, now rings.

"The suff'ring of our people when
In Egypt's land they called aloud,
You heard and signs and wonders sent
'Gainst Pharoah and his minions proud.

"For they and all their people had
Most arrogantly treated them.
Your name you honored, to this day
Exalted by the sons of Shem.

"The sea you parted that they might
Pass safely through while on dry land,
But Pharoah's men, pursuing, found
A watery grave by your command.

"By day you led them with a cloud,
A pillar's fire throughout the night,
And thus they knew the way to take,
So clearly brightened by the light.

"You spoke from heav'n at Sinai's peak,
Your just and righteous laws you gave,
Decrees, commandments only good,
To faithf'ly follow to the grave.

"Your holy Sabbath you made known,
Through Moses there you firmly spoke.
From heav'n you gave them daily bread
And their great hunger fully broke.

"They thirsted and you heard their cries,
From highest heav'n inclined your ear,
And water from the rock supplied,
Removing for a time their fear.

"Through Moses then you said to them,
'Now enter and possess the land
I promised to your fathers once,
And swore with my uplifted hand.'

"But arrogance our fathers knew,
And stiff-necked, chose to disobey.
They listened not, nor would recall
Your wonders of a bygone day.

"In their rebellion thus they chose
A leader who would guide them back
To Egypt where, though slaves, they thought
Their stomachs would no foodstuffs lack.

"But you are a forgiving God
Compassionate and full of grace,
Most slow to anger, filled with love,
And thus did not desert our race,

"Though they had cast a golden calf,
And said, 'This god has brought you out
From Egypt's land; now bend the knee,'
And further blasphemies would shout.

"Nor did you leave them to the sands
Of desert wastes, in righteous wrath.
By day the cloud, by night the fire
Ceased not to guide them 'long the path.

"You gave them your good Spirit that
He might instruct them in your way.
The manna you provided and
Sweet water for their thirst each day.

"And forty years you nourished them,
Their feet swelled not 'cross burning sands.
No wear upon their clothes was seen,
They nothing lacked 'spite heat's demands.

· JAMES VASQUEZ ·

"You gave them kingdoms, nations, to
The distant borders of some fame,
And Sihon, king of Heshbon with
The king of Bashan, Og by name.

"Their sons became as numerous
As stars the brilliant skies profess.
The land sworn to their fathers you
Bestowed, to enter and possess.

"Their sons, indeed, rose up to fight,
They entered and possessed the land.
And Canaan's people were subdued,
To suffer justice by their hand.

"Strong kings they took, their cities and
Their sheep and cattle in the fields,
The goods within their houses that
A quest for booty oft reveals.

"They took the wells, rich vineyards and
Tall groves of olive and of fruit.
Your sons ate well, their health increased,
Your goodness, Lord, none could dispute.

"Yet soon they disobeyed your law,
Rebellion in their midst was found.
Your words they put behind their backs,
And blasphemies fouled hallowed ground.

"They killed your prophets who were sent
To teach them well your holy ways,
That they once more might turn to you
And thus extend their halcyon days.

"And thus you gave them up to foes.
Oppression followed quickly, then.
But when they cried aloud to you,
Compassionate, you sent them men,

"Who from their bondage would set free,
That welcomed peace might then return.
But yet again they turned away,
Your kindness chose to boldly spurn.

"For evil done before your eyes,
You gave them up, abandoning
Your people to the enemy,
Who ruled with heartless prince and king.

"From heav'n you heard their pleas once more
And great in mercy, sent them aid.
And thus it was, time after time,
They called, you saved by bow and blade.

"You warned them much to keep decrees,
But arrogant, they chose to sin.
They flaunted laws for mankind's gain,
If faithfully they live within.

· JAMES VASQUEZ ·

"Both deaf and stiff-necked they became,
Admitting naught of how they erred.
Their backs they turned to you in pride.
All this with patience you endured.

"Then prophets, Spirit-filled, you sent,
To whom they paid but scant regard.
Their enemies once more rose up,
And left the land a waste and scarred.

"But in your mercy, great and free,
You did not put an end to them,
For grace and kindness, ever yours,
Did not allow their requiem.

"And now, O great and mighty God,
Most awesome in your deeds and thoughts,
Who keeps his covenant of love,
And kindness to his own allots,

"Let not our hardship be a thing
That as a trifling in your eyes,
May pass you quickly by, as one
Who without notice lives and dies.

"Our hardships weigh most heavily
Upon our kings, our leaders and
Our prophets, priests and fathers, found
In every place throughout the land.

"Yea, from those ancient days when kings
From yon Assyria ruled o'er us,
Until this very day we know
In all that happened, you are just.

"Most faithf'ly you have acted while
Uncounted times we chose the wrong,
Our kings, our leaders, fathers, priests,
Whose wicked deeds did guilt prolong.

"They followed not your law or ways,
To sane commands gave little heed,
Heard not the warnings from your lips,
Most kindly sent for our great need.

"Nor when within the promised land,
Enjoying fruit from every tree,
And your great goodness, did they turn
From all their sin and evil flee.

"Now see, we are but slaves today,
Within the land our fathers won,
That of its fruit and all good things
They might partake 'neath hearty sun.

"Yet for our sins, our harvests rich
To foreign kings belong this day.
By your decree they rule our beasts,
As well our bodies in their sway.

"And in our great distress for this,
A firm accord we herewith draw,
Our leaders, Levites and our priests
Their seals affix, and make it law."

Jonah Prays From the Depths

(Jnh 2:1-10)

Jonah disobeyed God when told to go to Nineveh "and preach against it." He boarded a ship to go in a different direction, to Tarshish possibly, on the coast of Spain. God sends a storm ("a great wind") and Jonah confesses to the sailors that he has sinned and was running away from "the God of heaven, who made the sea and the land." Terrified, and believing Jonah's disobedience has brought the violent storm, they finally accede to his suggestion and throw him overboard. Thence he prays:

From depths that only Sheol knows,
My life entwined with kelp,
To God in my distress I turned
And cried aloud for help.

The currents swirled about me then,
The waves swept over me.
They plunged me to the deepest pit
And thence he heard my plea.

"Though banished from your sight, yet I
Your holy temple will
Once more behold with lucid eye
Upon its sacred hill.

· James Vasquez ·

"My life was ebbing in the depths
But you remembered me,
And lifted me from deep within
The roiling, untamed sea.

"Now those who to their idols cling
Shall ne'er your goodness know,
For worthless will they find their prayers
And all your grace forgo.

"Salvation, Lord, alone with you
Is found in plenitude,
And thanks I'll give in sacrifice
With every vow renewed."

I found myself quite suddenly
Upon dry ground at last,
For God commanded that the fish
Continue on its fast,

Expelling me upon the shore
Where I once more would hear
The message that I first received,
Which caused me all my fear.

But I had learned through recent trials
And knew for sure that day,
That naught there was in life to fear
Except to disobey.

Habakkuk – "Though the Fig Tree Does Not Bud"

(HAB 1:2-4, 12-17; 3:1-19)

(1:2-4)

Habakkuk's first prayer (of several) is a complaint against God for his lack of activity in tolerating wrong in the land. A key phrase is the first one in the prayer: "How long, O Lord, must I call for help but you do not listen?"

How long, O Lord, will you not hear
The call for help I make?
How long will you not listen to
My voice for mercy's sake?

I cry to you, "What violence, Lord!"
And then behold no deed
That you have wrought or that you will
To save or even heed.

Injustice I am forced to see,
You tolerate the wrong.
Destruction and sheer violence
Distinguish every throng.

The law is paralyzed by strife
And justice ne'er prevails.
The wicked hem the righteous in
And conflict goodness veils.

(1:12-17)

Habakkuk continues complaining against God. Yet, he has learned, in answer to his first prayer, that God will bring the Babylonians to "sweep across the whole earth" and God will punish evil doers everywhere. Thus, he now asks, "Why are you silent while the wicked swallow up those more righteous than themselves?"

O Lord my God, are you not he
Of everlasting age?
My God, my Holy One, we will
Not die and leave earth's stage.

For they are destined by you, Lord,
To punish by your vow.
To execute your judgment they
Have been appointed now.

Too pure to look on evil are
Your eyes that see all things.
You will not tolerate the wrong
For malice that it brings.

Then why do you the treacherous
Endure for all their sin?
And why remain thus silent when
Such wicked men begin

To swallow up the righteous who
More honor have displayed
Than those you raise to punish us,
Who all their sin parade?

Like fish within the sea, you've made
All men and none to rule.
With hooks and net the enemy
Takes captive every school.

He gathers them, the net draws tight,
Rejoicing for his catch.
He sacrifices to his net
And incense burns to match.

By it he lives in luxury
And savors tasty food.
The choicest meats and wines are his
To satisfy his mood.

Will he continue with his net,
To empty it yet more?
Will he bring ruin to all men.
And mercy pleas ignore?

(3:1-19)

By this time it seems Habakkuk has learned to trust God's judgment and his sovereign, righteous ways. Verses three through seven are included in this prayer, though the text in these verses speaks of God in the third person. They fit perfectly in the prayer that precedes and follows those verses. The book ends with the famous declaration by Habakkuk that "Though the fig tree does not bud and there are no grapes on the vines . . . yet I will rejoice in the Lord, I will be joyful in God my Savior."

Your fame, O Lord, has filled my ear,
In awe your deeds I scan,
In wrath remember mercy, Lord,
And in our life's brief span,

· James Vasquez ·

Renew your marvels, make them known
To us midst all our fright,
As when in glory you appeared
From distant Teman's height.

Like sunrise was your splendor then,
And flashing from your hand
Effulgent rays in vain concealed
The power you e'er command.

Such glory all the heavens veiled
While praises filled the earth.
Before you plague and pestilence
Brought famine, blight and dearth.

You stood, the earth was shaken well,
You looked, the nations feared,
And mountains of a hoary age
And hills then disappeared.

The tents of Cushan cried aloud
And Midian's dwellings wailed.
Your ways from all eternity
Have ever, Lord, prevailed.

But were you angry with the streams?
'Gainst rivers was your wrath?
And was it with the sea you raged
When on your conquering path

You ventured forth with chariot
And rode upon the horse,
O'er waves while calling for your bow
And arrows on your course?

The earth by rivers' flood was split
And waves were lifted high,
While deep roared unto boundless deep
And mounts did writhe and sigh.

The heav'ns were stilled by sun and moon
Beholding flashing spear,
And glint of arrows you unleashed
That traced their passage near.

The nations then were threshed anew,
The earth in wrath you strode.
You came your people to redeem,
Th' anointed one's abode.

The leader of the wicked you
Then crushed and stripped him well.
And with his spear you pierced his head
Who tottered there and fell,

Just as his gloating warriors rushed
To scatter us abroad
From where we fled to hide ourselves,
In cave or field or sod.

· James Vasquez ·

Your horses, Lord, the raging sea
Their trampling hooves subdued,
While churning waters violently
For their belligerent mood.

My lips then quivered and my heart
Beat louder at the sound.
Decay beset my bones, my legs
In trembling plight were found.

And I for all will yet await
And patiently abide,
Till great calamity shall turn
Th' invading foe aside.

And though the fig tree will not bloom,
The vine bears naught of grape,
The olive only failure yields,
Each field a barren scape,

No sheep within the pen are found
Nor cattle in the stall,
Yet in my God will I rejoice
As on him I shall call.

My strength is in the Sovereign Lord,
My feet as from a deer
He makes to bear me swift above,
And on the heights appear.

· JAMES VASQUEZ ·

Jesus, Man of Prayer

(Lᴋ)

It is ironic that the man in Scripture we would think had the least need for prayer in his life, prayed the most. Yes, Jesus was a man of prayer. He rose early in the morning to pray (Mk 1:35), he spent all night in prayer (Lk 6:12), he prayed when alone (Mk 1:35), he prayed before meals (Mk 6:41). He prayed before such critical moments as choosing the twelve apostles (Lk 6:12-13), before Peter's recognition of him as the Messiah (Lk 9:18), and during the Transfiguration when God affirmed he was His Son in words the three apostles heard (Lk 9:28). He was praying when the apostles (finally) asked him to teach them to pray (Lk 11:1), and when facing the cross, which at first he resisted (Lk 22:42). His last words on the cross were prayers (Lk 23:46; Mt 27:46).

Jesus also taught his followers how not to pray: not babbling (Mt 6:7), not just to be heard by others (Mt 6:5), not with many words (Mt 6:7), not dwelling on their own righteousness (Lk 18:11), and not imitating the pagans (Mt 6:5).

The following poem won the Master Poet Award in Poet's Pen, *Dr Charles McCravey, ed., Sum 2008.*

Through many years I sought them out,
I questioned and then listened well.
By day, by night I walked or rode
Wherever they might work or dwell,

For tales had reached me of a man
Who wandered throughout Israel's tribes,
Unlike the sages of our lore,
Long penned by Greece's fertile scribes.

Belov'd physician, I was called,
Yet I had left this practice now,
In search of one who could, they said,
Some respite for my soul allow,

For what I learned about this man
Would put my bothered heart at ease.
It spoke to my most urgent need,
Far graver than some mere disease.

Perhaps the time will come when I,
With pen in hand and parchment spread,
Will write the things I learned of him,
This Jesus but, for now instead,

Please join me on this oaken bench,
Your ear will have to serve me well.
Gaze far into the endless sky
And hear this tale I have to tell.

Yes, witnesses I sought who walked
And talked with him each passing day,
Who heard his words and saw his deeds,
Who ate with him and saw him pray.

He raised the dead and healed the sick,
He fed the hungry all about.
He cleansed the temple of its beasts
And money changers rooted out.

He toyed with experts in the Law,
Exposing them as fools they were.
He bested priests at every turn
And suffered many'a vile slur.

And when I was quite satisfied
I'd heard from many, young and old,
I set myself to thinking which,
Of all the things that I'd been told,

Impressed me most about the man,
This Jesus whose blest life I traced,
I came to one most startling fact
Which I most strongly then embraced.

'Twas not the miracles he did,
Beyond our understanding sure,
Like casting demons to the ground
Or healing sickness mongst the poor,

Nor was it raising from the dead
Departed souls with but a word,
Or yet the winds and waves he calmed
When all their fury he deferred.

No, it was this, most simply put,
That I with you now gladly share:
For from each dawn to close of day
This Jesus was a man of prayer.

A look of doubt, of unbelief,
Do I detect upon your face?
Then hear me out and surely I
Your deep misgivings will erase.

'Twas said of him, I heard if oft,
That long before the light of day
He went alone atop a hill
And sat himself that he might pray.

At times he spent a night in prayer,
Before he took a meal he prayed.
His final words were but a prayer,
And from this need he never strayed.

Now listen as I tell you how
The Father honored every plea,
For countless are the things transpired
When Jesus prayed, as you will see.

The heavens opened on the day
From Jordan's waters Jesus prayed,
And this submissive deed of his
The Father's highest tribute bade.

He spent a night upon his knees
And in the morning chose the twelve
To follow him as loyal friends,
Though one in treacherous schemes would delve.

He prayed and Peter then confessed
He was the Christ, God's only Son.
He prayed and then five thousand fed,
And gathered much when they were done.

He prayed upon a mount and then
The heav'ns themselves at once were rent.
A Voice affirmed he was God's Son,
To bring good news to sinners sent.

His followers finally asked that he
Might teach them how to pray aright.
Now surely, this he long had hoped,
That they, at last, would see the light.

It happened on a day when he
Was quite alone in prayer, as wont,
And what he taught has ever been
For all our prayers a boundless font.

He taught us to begin a prayer
Addressing Him as Father, who
O'er all our needs each day presides,
To whom all veneration's due.

Now much there is to say I've not
Revealed though you have listened well.
We should not babble when we pray,
Nor on our goodness proudly dwell.

In secret should our prayers be said,
But not on corners where crowds are.
And ever should we ask to be
From all temptation led afar.

But now your gracious leave I beg,
A friend I'll join, and have for years.
By river's edge we clasp our hands
And raise our voice to him who hears.

Mary's Song

(Lk 1:46–55)

Mary apparently spoke these words of praise while visiting her cousin Elizabeth in the hill country of Judea. When she entered the residence and greeted Elizabeth she heard her cousin bless her as "the mother of my Lord" and for believing "what the Lord has said to her will be accomplished!" Although properly a song of praise rather than a prayer addressed to God, it is included here because it teaches much about praise in our own prayers.

She heard the angel voice announce
A child she was to bear,
Whose kingdom would no end discern
As David's royal heir.

And blest was she mongst women for
God favored her so well,
And Virgin Mary then began
This song of praise to tell:

My soul now magnifies the Lord,
For mindful of my state
And all my lowly circumstance
That e'er have been my fate,

He has requited mercif'ly
And great things he has done.
My name will generations bless,
Their voices raise as one.

· James Vasquez ·

His Name is holy and in him
My spirit will rejoice,
My Savior God, the Mighty One,
Whose praise this day I voice.

To those who fear him mercy shall
Their portion ever be,
But those who harbor pride within
He scatters mightily.

And rulers mongst the nations he
From thrones has now brought down,
But kindly does he look on those
Of humble, meek renown.

The hungry has he filled and more
With good things they required,
And empty sent the rich away,
Nor gave what they desired.

His servant Israel he has
Remembered mercif'ly.
And kindness has he shown to those
Of Abr'ham's progeny.

Zechariah's Song

(Lk 1:67-79)

Zechariah's song of praise follows the birth of his long-awaited son, John. The baby's mother and father both insisted, against the cultural norm and others who came to circumcise the child, that he was to be named John and not Zechariah, after his father. This naming of John opened the father's mouth, which had remained silent since the appearance of the angel Gabriel, who announced Elizabeth would give birth to his son. Zechariah had doubted the angel's words. As with Mary's Song, this song of praise adds to our knowledge of praise in prayer.

And Zechariah prophesied
As those of old were wont to do,
For with the Spirit he was filled
And thus his words rang true.

"Praise be to God, the Lord of all,
Of Israel whom he has redeemed,
Who now to David's noble house
His servant most esteemed,

"Has come and kindly raised for us
Salvation's horn as long ago
Was told by holy prophets that
Deliverance we might know,

"From all our enemies and from
The hand of those who hate us well,
That mercy to our fathers he
Might show and we might tell.

"Thus to remember all his oath,
The holy covenant he swore,
To Abraham our father that
Our fortunes he'd restore,

"And from the hand of enemies
He'd rescue us and grant that we
Might serve him in all righteousness,
And from all fear be free.

"And you, my child, of God Most High,
A prophet shall be called one day,
For you shall go before the Lord
And shall prepare his way,

"The knowledge of salvation shall
You give his people, and their sin
Through God's most tender mercy shall
His full forgiveness win,

"By which the rising sun will come
From heav'n and brightly shine on those
In darkness and death's shadow that
In peace they might repose."

This Favor Over All

(Jn 2; Mt 21)

More speculative than other poems in this book, the events here described must certainly have occurred many times among women (and men) who sought a quiet place for prayer in the temple but did not find it. At least, not until God saw their plight and opened the way for what they so earnestly desired.

I early rise this misty dawn
And wake my children from their sleep,
That to the temple we may haste,
Our vigil there to keep.

An hour spent in prayer with God
Begins our harried day so well,
And hope we gain to do his will
And in his presence dwell.

Now countless are the times that hour
Ere I had risen to depart
Removed the pain and burdens from
My sad, despairing heart.

And would another hour or two
I had to kneel and linger there,
To sing, to praise or simply wait
Most quietly in prayer.

· James Vasquez ·

But widows must the time redeem
And vigilantly search each day,
That food for children's stomachs might
Be found and served some way.

But 'twas not always that we came
And found a corner calm, serene,
Where mother, son and daughter could
A moment's blessing glean.

For once within the temple courts
A desecrating mess was found,
With money changers at their seats
And birds and beasts around.

And merchants called as I my way
Would wend in hopes to pass them by.
They offered cattle, lamb or sheep
And for my coin would cry.

And such the raucous, hawking noise,
As they their profane wares would laud,
Quite hopeless was my quest to find
A tranquil place with God.

How much I owe that man who came
And raised his voice for what he saw,
And with a fashioned whip in hand
Put each of them in awe.

For as his whip upon their backs
Brought anguished cries of pain and woe,
They scurried from the presence of
That angry, violent foe.

He routed money changers and
Their laden tables overturned,
And none had courage to oppose
For well his wrath they earned.

"This house a house of prayer shall be
As once my Father did avow,
And not a den of robbers as
Your deeds have made it now!"

And with these words he drove them out,
Nor have they dared return as yet,
Such zeal consumed him for God's house
He thus their deeds beset.

· James Vasquez ·

Now many'a day I've thought of him
For word of other signs is told,
As he among our people dwells
And they his works behold.

Much good he's done in every way,
But I this favor over all
Will cherish well beyond each one
As on the Lord I call,

Within the temple's quiet gates
Where once again on holy sod,
With humble praise and thankful heart
I seek and find my God.

The Lord's Prayer

(Mt 6:5-13; Lk 11:2-4)

This prayer is the supreme example of prayer in the Bible; millions of followers of Jesus Christ repeat this prayer in unison every Sunday while in church. With reason, for it contains virtually all the critical elements of prayer: acknowledgement of God's holiness, submission to his will, profession of dependence on Him for daily sustenance, confession of sin and obligation to forgive others, admission of weakness in the presence of temptation and plea for protection from Satan. No other prayer in so few words has ever surpassed it in completeness. Midst an extended sermon on a mountainside, the Lord gave this prayer to his disciples and "the crowds," if they had in fact joined the disciples by that time.

"Then in this manner lift your voice
To praise him or beseech,
If you would speak to God and know
Your prayer the heavens reach.

"'As Father now we call on you
And hallowed is your name.
In heav'n you dwell eternally,
From you creation came.

"'May your bright kingdom come at last,
Your will be done by all,
On earth as throughout heaven 'tis
By ruler, subject, thrall.

"'Our bread this day now grant us that
Our needs be fully met.
Forgive us each offense as we
Forgive each man his debt.

"'Let not the tempter's dark intrigues
Ensnare us in the way,
But from the evil one preserve
Our fallen souls this day.'

"Forgiving thus another when
He sins against you well,
Your Father will forgive your sins
And all your guilt dispel.

"But choosing not forgiveness you
Shall not forgiveness know
From him whose love you've tasted and
To whom all things you owe."

The Friend at Midnight

(Lk 11:5-10)

It is usually thought that the basic teaching of this passage is on persistence in prayer, (or boldness as the NIV has it in the text). It is clear that the contrast between a selfish "friend" and a generous, attentive Father in heaven is also portrayed. In the Luke passage this parable immediately follows the Lord's Prayer.

And then to teach a further truth
Concerning how one ought to pray,
Our Lord this parable invoked,
His followers' question to allay.

"Suppose a friend of yours lacks bread
With which a visitor to feed,
And thus at midnight he appears
And wakes a neighbor for his need.

"'Friend, have you bread?' he asks of him.
'Perhaps three loaves that you might loan.
A visitor has come to me,
And none I have that is my own.'

"The neighbor answers he cannot
This friend's request grant or allow.
'The door is locked, my children sleep,
There's naught that I can give you now.'

"Though not for friendship will he rise
And give the man all he desires,
Yet for his boldness he'll agree
Before the dark of night expires.

"And thus I say to you, but ask,
For it shall then be given you.
And seeking you will surely find,
And all that you have sought accrue.

"The door is opened to the one
Who knocks and then will knock again,
For as good gifts you grant your sons,
So will the Father treat all men."

My Yoke is Easy

(Mt 11:25-30)

It is noteworthy that these words of Jesus follow upon the heels of a passage in which he pronounces the most extreme woe on cities that did not repent when they beheld the miracles done in them, presumably by Jesus himself. Their punishment will be worse than that which befell Sodom. In spite of the people's rejection of his message, Jesus here invites the "weary and burdened" to come to him and find rest.

'Twas then that Jesus raised his voice,
"I praise you, Father, Lord of all
In heav'n and earth, wherever found,
Each woman, man you call.

"For from the learned of this world,
And those who hail themselves as wise,
These truths of judgment and amends
You've hidden from their eyes,

"Which unto children are revealed.
By such is your true wisdom known,
For to the innocent and pure
Is your great pleasure shown.

"And all things by my Father have
Been giv'n the Son in his domains.
For none may know the Son but he
Who as the Father reigns.

· James Vasquez ·

"Nor shall one know the Father but
The Son, and those to whom he may
Reveal the Father's glory and
His majesty display.

"Oh! come, you weary, burdened well,
To me now come and find your rest.
My yoke assume and learn from me,
Draw near at my behest,

"For with a gentle, humble heart,
I bid you for your soul's delight,
Find rest; my yoke is easy and
My burden wholly light."

A Secret Long Pursued

(Lk 18:1-8)

This is another passage that teaches much about prayer though not containing a prayer. The contrast once more is between a merciless man (a judge) who "neither feared God nor cared about men," and a God who is caring and just in all his ways.

How strangely weak his followers were,
Enduring not in trial,
And ready soon to quit the fight
Nor walk the second mile.

This parable then Jesus gave
That they might always strive
In prayer to God who ever seeks
Our spirits to revive.

"A certain judge who feared not God
Nor cared for man's estate,
Was daily by a widow vexed,
At dawn, noontide and late.

"'Now grant me justice,' was her plea,
'Against my lawless foe,
And my condition please review,
Some retribution show.'

"And for a while his ear was deaf
To all her urgency,
For naught he cared of God or man
And less this widow's plea.

"But then the day arrived when he,
His patience at an end,
And near exhaustion turned about
Her pleading to attend.

"'Unless I hear this woman's case
She'll not her suit forgo.
She'll hound me to a certain death
And peace I'll never know.'"

And Jesus paused a moment then,
And to his followers said,
"Now hear this unjust man's reply
To what the woman pled.

"And will not God so caring and
So just in all his ways,
Be quick to hear his chosen ones
Who call throughout their days,

"For justice 'gainst their enemies
And those who do them wrong?
Will he not swiftly judgment bring,
Nor pause nor tarry long?

"For God, unlike this spiteful judge,
The lowly stoops to hear,
Delighting when they raise their voice
To lend his kindly ear."

And with this final word the Lord
To every listener there
Revealed the secret, long pursued,
For God to answer prayer.

"And when the Son of Man," he said,
"Appears on earth again,
Will he though searching far and wide
Find faith among all men?"

The Pharisee and the Tax Collector

(Lк 18:9–14)

Two prayers are uttered here by two men and the contrast could not be greater.
The Pharisee's prayer contains thirty-three words, the tax collector's but seven.
But even greater contrast is found in the content, for the one prayer is longer
because the Pharisee needed more words to convey all his righteousness to God.
The tax collector's prayer is brief because he needed few words to express his
unworthiness.

Now some there were with heads held high,
Quite righteous in their view,
Of who they thought themselves to be.
They stood among the few.

And since they looked askance at men
Whom they considered less,
This parable the Lord then spoke,
Their manner to redress.

"Two men went to the temple and
Each prayed as best he thought.
The Pharisee stood tall and straight
And thanked God he was not

"Akin to other men who stole,
Did evil deeds and more.
Adult'ry he did not commit
And other sins forswore.

· James Vasquez ·

122

"'Nor am I like this shameful man
Who stands behind me now.
I fast each week and from what's mine,
A tenth to God allow.'

"The tax collector from afar
Would not so much as look
Above to heav'n, which he quite feared,
And all pretense forsook.

"'Have mercy on me now, dear God,
A sinner,' he confessed.
He kept his eyes quite downward still,
And beat upon his breast.

"I tell you this man left the place
In God's eyes justified,
And not the Pharisee who prayed
In words so filled with pride.

"For those who will exalt themselves
Shall find a lowly place,
But he of humble circumstance
Much honor will embrace."

That They May Believe

(Jɴ 11:41-44)

Jesus here affirms that one of the reasons he performed miraculous signs was that others would believe he was sent by the Father. No doubt another reason was simply that he had mercy on the one on whom the miracle was performed. Both reasons were present in raising Lazarus from the dead. Though he knew the Father always heard his prayers, he particularly thanks Him for hearing his prayer in this passage.

The stone was removed at his word,
And Jesus looked up to the sky,
"I thank you, dear Father, you heard
My plea that ascended on high.

"Yea, Father, I know that you hear
Each prayer that my heart renders true,
Nor ever dismiss any plea,
I humbly may offer to you.

"But this I have said for the crowd,
That round me has gathered this day,
That they may believe you have sent
Both me and the words that I say."

And turning to face the mute tomb,
He called in a voice clear and loud,
"Come Lazarus, out from your bed,
And leave your cold darkness and shroud."

Then forth came his friend from the dead,
Yet wrapped well his hands and his feet.
"Now loose and receive him as yore,
This man who death's call would defeat."

Jesus' Prayer for His Followers

(JN 17)

This is easily the longest of our Lord's recorded prayers. He prays not only for the disciples in his day, but for "those who will believe in me through their message, that all of them may be one." Jesus first prays for himself and various petitions follow.

With eyes cast upward Jesus prayed
To Him who dwells above,
And ne'er were heard such words before
Of longing, hope and love.

The time, my Father, has arrived,
Bring glory to your Son,
That his may be reflected back
And yours with his be one.

For over people everywhere
He has authority,
That he might grant eternal life
By your divine decree.

And this is life eternal that
They know the one true God,
And Jesus Christ whom you have sent,
And in alliance laud.

The work you gave for me to do
I have completed now,
And glory thus redounds to you,
If earthly works allow.

And in your presence grant that I
My glory now may find,
Just as to me ere earth was formed,
In heaven was consigned.

And these surrounding me have you
Now given to my hand,
For long before this gift they were
The chosen in the land.

The glories of your Name have I
To them at length displayed,
And from the world you took them, for
Your word they have obeyed.

And all that you have given me,
Which they have seen and heard,
They know proceeds from you, as I
Have given them your word.

And thus they know with certainty
That I was sent by you,
I pray for these, though not the world,
For they are poor and few.

· James Vasquez ·

And all I have on earth is yours
Throughout its length and girth,
While all in heaven that is yours
Is mine as well on earth.

And glory has to me accrued
Through these who have believed,
For they have put their lives aright
And suff'ring have perceived.

No longer shall my dwelling place
Within the world remain,
For soon will I ascend to heav'n
And take my rightful reign.

O Holy Father, keep them by
The power of your Name,
The Name to me once given that
Their oneness be the same,

As that which I with you have shared
Throughout eternity,
For, dwelling in their midst, they are
Most safely kept by me.

And none was ever lost—save he
Who Scripture prophesied
Would find destruction as his end,
And justice satisfied.

· JAMES VASQUEZ ·

To you I come but first to them
These things while here I say,
That all the fullness of my joy
Be with them now and aye.

Your word I gave and thus the world
Has hated them, for they
Are not its children just as I
Live not within its sway.

I pray not that they be removed
From every trial and care,
For that would mean from out the world
You transport them elsewhere.

No, let them here remain a while
And of earth's woes partake,
While by your mighty hand you keep
Nor e'er their lives forsake.

And by your word of truth may they
Be fully sanctified,
And thus, devoted to your use,
In holiness abide.

For as I came into the world
First sent by your decree,
So now I send these men that they
My witnesses may be.

· JAMES VASQUEZ ·

And that their lives in all things may
Bring honor to your Name,
I sanctify my very self
And full devotion claim.

And not for these alone I pray
But those who shall believe,
When hearing what they tell of me
And to their message cleave,

That those with these may truly be
But one in heart and mind,
As you, dear Father, within me
And I in you do find.

And may my foll'wers ever dwell
In us with full assent,
That worldly souls may understand
By you I first was sent.

The glory that you gave me have
I given them that they,
As we are one, their unity
May faithfully display.

And thus the world will surely know
That as your love for me,
So also is your love to them
And will forever be.

Now grant that these, your gifts to me,
Be ever by my side,
That they my glory may behold,
By heaven testified,

Which ere the world was founded you
To me in love assigned,
In hopes all men its end would seek
And every man would find.

For well, O Righteous Father, have
I known just who you are,
And though the world may know you not,
If near or yet afar,

My own are now persuaded that
From you I did proceed,
For I have made you known to them
By every word and deed.

And that your love to me remain
In them, I ever will
Continue to reveal yourself
And their awareness fill,

And thus will I within each one,
My foll'wer first and last,
Most joyful take my long-sought place
Till earth's brief years are past.

· JAMES VASQUEZ ·

A Thief's Final Prayer

(Lᴋ 23:40-43)

*The last words of several men facing death in Scripture were prayers: Samson,
Jesus, Stephen, and the thief in this passage. Apparently the thief studied Jesus
for a while on the cross. He came to the conclusion that this was no ordinary
man; rather, he was the Son of God who one day would return to establish his
kingdom. The thief prays he will be remembered on that day.*

And suddenly I am aware,
(As day turns into night!)
I've known no other love so true,
Or truth that shone so bright.

No mortal, he, who hangs beside,
Less rebel, martyr, thief,
But One who over all has reign
And merits my belief.

Is this to be one final chance
That fate has offered me?
Will he who hangs upon the cross
Accept my one last plea?

I thirst! But now 'tis not for drink
The body does require,
'Tis now my soul athirst for Him
With burning, deep desire.

And in my helplessness I cry,
"Remember me the day
You come into your kingdom, Lord,
And all your power display."

He looks upon me as he says,
"For this meek Sacrifice,
I tell you that today you'll be
With me in Paradise."

And now my thirst is gone at last,
My shadowy eyes have sight,
My soul that long in darkness dwelt
Perceives the end of night.

Believers' Prayer

(ACTS 4:23–31)

Peter and John had just been released from prison by the Sanhedrin, who feared punishing them further because, "Everybody in Jerusalem knows they have done an outstanding miracle, and we cannot deny it." After threatening them again they released the two. The apostles went to "their own people" and told them all that had happened. As one, the people raised their voices in prayer.

When Peter and his brother John
From prison walls were then released,
At once they joined their faithful friends,
Whose apprehension quickly ceased.

Recounting to their brethren what
With priests and elders had occurred,
They brought great joy to all and thus
This prayer, as with one voice, was heard:

"O Sovereign Lord, the heav'ns you made,
The earth, the sea and all within,
Who by the Spirit spoke these words
Through David, father and our kin,

"'Why do the angry nations rage?
The restive peoples plot in vain?
The kings of earth now take their stand
With rulers gathered where they reign.

"'Against the Lord they've taken arms
Throughout each base, rebellious land,
'Gainst him whose praises prophets sang,
Th' Anointed One by God's own hand.'

"Both Pilate and King Herod met
With Israel and with Gentiles too,
To plot against your servant and
Conspire his favor to undo.

"They did but what your power and
Your will determined should be done.
Now look upon their threats, O Lord,
And may their triumphs thus be none.

"May we with boldness speak your word,
While by your outstretched hands are done
True healings, signs and wonders through
The name of Jesus, your blest Son."

The place was greatly shaken when
On God in prayer they ceased to call.
With God's own Spirit they were filled
And boldly spoke his word to all.

Paul's Thorn in the Flesh

(2 Co 12:7-10)

*Paul's plea that God would remove the "thorn" in his flesh is a remarkable
snapshot from his life, as it is one of the few times he acknowledges that God
does not answer all of his prayers, at least not as he prayed God would. Yet, he
recognizes it is for his good and subsequently exclaims, "I will boast all the more
gladly about my weaknesses . . . For when I am weak, then I am strong."*

Yea, brethren, every day I faced
A vile conceit quite warmly fanned,
For all the revelations giv'n,
By God's most gracious hand.

A messenger the Lord then sent
From Satan—in my flesh a thorn!
Tormenting me throughout each night,
And by first light of morn.

Three times I knelt and pleaded that
The Lord remove this thorn from me,
That some relief I might obtain,
And hoped he heard my plea.

And surely, then, he heard my voice,
He answered finally, firm and clear,
But said there'd be no kind release,
Though I had sought it dear.

He further said,—I'll not forget—,
"My grace is most sufficient, for
In weakness all its power finds,
My strength thus to outpour."

And so will I boast all the more
Of weaknesses within me found,
That Christ's great strength may rest on me,
And power divine abound.

For his sake, then, I take delight
In trials and weakness every hour,
In persecution and distress,
For weak, I gain his power.

Paul's Prayer for the Ephesians

(Eph 1:15-23)

Though not a prayer in itself, in this passage Paul informs the Ephesians just how and for what he prays for them. His persistence and heart-felt concern are evident several times in such phrases as, "I have not stopped giving thanks for you," "I (remember) you in my prayers," "I keep asking that . . . God . . . may give you the Spirit of wisdom," and "I pray also . . ."

Through faith in Christ, dear brethren, we
May boldly come to God in prayer,
With confidence and freedom our
Most ardent heart's desire to bare.

'Tis for this reason that I kneel
Before the Father, from whom we,
His family both in heav'n and earth,
Derive our name by his decree.

I pray that from his riches, he
May strengthen you with glorious power,
Through his blest Spirit dwelling in
Your inner being every hour,

That Christ may dwell within your hearts,
And firm in love, established well,
You may with saints wherever found,
Have power to grasp his love and tell

How wide and long, how high and deep
The love of Christ his deeds display,
A love excelling knowledge and
Which guards his people now and aye,

That you to all the measure of
God's fullness may be daily filled,
And thus complete with joy each task
His boundless love for you has willed.

To him most able to do far
Beyond what we can think or know,
By his unmeasured power in us,
As wondrous works each hour now show,

Be glory in the church this day
And in Christ Jesus, now and e'er,
Through his abounding riches and
His glorious might beyond compare.

Created By Your Will

(Rev 4:8-11)

While "in the Spirit" John is caught up into heaven and witnesses "living creatures" and "twenty-four elders" before the throne of God, in worship and prayer. This is the first of five such experiences John would have in heaven.

Four living creatures round the throne,
Each boasted six bright, flowing wings,
With eyes that covered them throughout.
And day and night their descant rings;

"Most holy, holy, holy is
The Lord Almighty, one true God,
Who was, who is, who is to come,
As angel voices ever laud."

And when the living creatures give
All glory, honor, thanks to him,
Who sits upon th' exalted throne,
Whose worthiness the angels limn,

Of elders twenty-four fall down
Before him, all in bright array.
They offer up their golden crowns
And lifting radiant eyes, they say,

"Our Lord and God, most worthy you,
Of glory, honor and of power.
By you creation was ordained,
All things existing to this hour.

"You spoke the word and gave them form,
By wisdom and a gracious will,
Their being wholly owed to you,
They stand as testimony still."

Worthy Is the Lamb Once Slain

(Rev 5:9-14)

While the passage in chapter four appears to center on God the Father as Creator, in chapter five the focus is on Jesus, who "was slain, and with your blood you purchased men for God from every tribe and language and people and nation." Here, it is angels "numbering thousands upon thousands" who proclaim the Lamb's worthiness, followed by "every creature in heaven and on earth, and under the earth and on the sea," who raise their voices in praise to "him who sits on the throne and to the Lamb."

They sang a new song, elders and
The living creatures prostrate there.
Before the Lamb upon the throne,
They offered him this praise-filled prayer,

"Most worthy now to take the scroll
Are you, its seals to open wide,
For you were slain and purchased men
With blood from your once-riven side.

"For God you bought them from each tribe
And language, people, near and far.
You made of them a kingdom and
High priests, as God's true servants are."

I looked again and heard the voice
Of myriad angels, whose great sum
Beyond my counting quite surpassed,
And I was nearly overcome.

The angels stood around the throne,
And round the elders, creatures, too.
Their voices tuned aloud to sing
This chant, this laud, this praise anew;

"Oh, worthy is the Lamb once slain,
All power, wealth and wisdom now,
With strength and honor, glory, praise,
To own, before whom all must bow."

Then creatures found throughout the heav'ns,
On earth, in depths beneath the sea,
And all within them in accord,
This hymn proclaimed with spirits free,

"To him who sits upon the throne,
And to the Lamb at his blest side,
Be praise and honor, glory, power,
Beyond all years the heav'ns abide."

The living creatures spoke but this,
"Amen," affirming every word.
The elders fell upon their knees,
In full assent to all they heard.

· JAMES VASQUEZ ·

The Kingdom of Our Lord

(Rev 11:15-19)

John moves forward in his account of the victory Christ bought and the subsequent reign of God, leading to judgment of the dead ("who destroy the earth"). He now speaks of the rewarding of his servants the prophets, the saints and those who reverence his Name, "both small and great." The praise is sung by the twenty-four elders and "loud voices in heaven."

Aloud the trumpet sounded as
The seventh angel blew his horn,
In heav'n bold voices then were heard,
To cause rejoicing, others warn.

"The kingdom of the world has now
Become the kingdom of our Lord,
And of his Christ, who shall for e'er
Reign over men with just reward."

The elders seated on their thrones,
Fell on their faces worshipping
The God before whom they lay prone,
Nor would they cease their praise to bring.

"We give you thanks, Lord God of all,
Who is and was in times long past,
For you have taken your great power,
And thus begun to reign at last.

"For angry were the nations when
Your fearful wrath upon them came.
Yea, now has come the time for men,
    Alive or dead, regardless fame,

"To stand before you and be judged,
For prophets and your servants who,
With saints your name revere, to know
Reward for lives resolved and true.

"But those quite bent on earth's demise,
Will be destroyed themselves the day
You bring before your judgment seat,
All peoples and their deeds repay."

God's temple in the heav'ns was then
Most widely opened, and within,
The ark of his great cov'nant with
The blood that covered all men's sin,

Was seen by all with open eye,
As lightning flashed all round about,
With thunder, earthquake, pelting hail
That left of God's great wrath no doubt.

Song of the Lamb

(Rev 15:2-4)

The saints, "who had been victorious over the beast and his image," harps in hand, sing these words of praise to the "Lord God Almighty . . . King of the ages."

And then I saw what looked to be
A sea of glass all mixed with fire,
And standing by, all persons who
O'ercame the beast and his great ire.

They conquered, too, his image and
His most inglorious, treach'rous name,
As well the numbers given him,
For which he gained much odious fame.

Their hands embraced gold harps from God,
The song of Moses they intoned,
That servant of the Lord Most High,
Who Israel's fortunes once had owned.

I heard them sing with unbound voice,
The Lamb's Song who, forever praised,
Himself once offered on the cross,
And thus the path to heaven blazed.

"Your deeds are marv'lous, Lord, this day,
And great beyond all words and thought.
Your ways both just and true for e'er,
O King of ages, heav'n begot.

"What man is there who fears you not,
Or fails to offer glory now?
The Holy One alone you are,
To whom all faithfulness we vow.

"The nations will in worship come
Before you, and exalt your name,
For now your acts of righteousness
Have been revealed to man's acclaim."

· James Vasquez ·

You Are Just

(Rev 16:4-7)

As if to bring a conclusion to these end-of-time pronouncements, it is finally angels who proclaim the truth and justice of all God's judgments, joined by "the altar," probably referring to "the souls (under the altar) of those who had been slain because of the word of God and the testimony they had maintained" in Rev 6:9, where their theme is God's judgment to come.

Upon the rivers and the springs
The third of angels poured his bowl,
To blood they quickly turned throughout,
From end to end, in part and whole.

And one who charge of waters owned,
Spoke words that all my soul would stir,
"Most just in every judgment, Lord,
Are you who are and ever were,

"The Holy One who has so judged
The men who saints and prophets slew.
They now receive their just reward,
And blood to drink, which is their due."

And then the altar answered clear,
"Yea, Lord of all, th' Almighty God,
For true and just your judgments e'er,
And worthy of all praise and laud."

· James Vasquez ·